KHWEZI

KHWEZI

· · · · · · · ·

The Story of Fezekile Ntsukela Kuzwayo

Redi Tlhabi

Jonathan Ball Publishers

JOHANNESBURG & CAPE TOWN

© Text Redi Tlhabi, 2017
© Published edition, Jonathan Ball Publishers, 2017
Reprinted once in 2017

First published in South Africa in 2017 by
JONATHAN BALL PUBLISHERS
A division of Media24 (Pty) Ltd
PO Box 33977
Jeppestown
2043

ISBN 978-1-86842-726-0
ebook ISBN 978-1-86842-727-7

*Every effort has been made to trace the copyright holders and to obtain their permission
for the use of copyright material. The publishers apologise for any errors or omissions
and would be grateful to be notified of any corrections that should be incorporated in
future editions of this book.*

All photos courtesy of Fezekile Kuzwayo's friends and family, except for pp. 7, 177, 187
Marc Wegerif, p. 88 (top) Eva-Lotta Jansson/Alamy Stock Photo, p. 88 (bottom) and p. 89
ALEXANDER JOE/AFP/Getty Images, p. 213 and p. 248 Teresa Yates, and p. 212 and
back cover Gallo Images/Deon Raath.

Twitter: www.twitter.com/JonathanBallPub
Facebook: www.facebook.com/JonathanBallPublishers
Blog: http://jonathanball.bookslive.co.za/

Cover by publicide
Front cover image of Khwezi in Marangu in the foothills of Kilimanjaro © Marc Wegerif
Design and typesetting by Triple M Design
Printed and bound by CTP Printers, Cape Town
Set in 11/17pt Times

. . . .

Contents

Dear Fez, this is not the book I had in mind;
you left too soon, while we were still talking.
But in these pages, you live on, triumphant, beautiful and positive.
Rest in peace …

MaBeauty – life has been hard, but still you live and fight.

Big thank you to all Fezeka's friends, Shaun, Prudence, Lungi,
Auntie Bunie, Wisani, Teresa, Marc, Kay, Allan and Danielle,
all of whom went beyond the requirements of friendship.

Fezeka's friends in Amsterdam, who gave her a new tomorrow.

Her family, Zintle, Nokuzola, Ntsikelelo.

My husband Brian – it is always hard for you when I write,
but you cheer me on. Thank you.

. . . .

Prologue

Durban, 15 October 2016

I am stunned. Broken.

Here I am, attending a funeral instead of a triumphant book launch.

We had imagined the scene so many times: the exultation we would feel at the launch when she showed her face to the world, told her story and reclaimed her name. She was adamant – she would attend the launch and I was to introduce her by her real name. In one of our conversations, she had told me with admirable defiance: 'The rapist is not hiding. Why must I? Khwezi has served me well, but now it is time for her to go.'

I believed her: months before her death, I sent her two books by courier. I asked her to whom I should address the package.

'To me,' she answered.

'No, I mean, should I use your public name – Khwezi – or something else?'

She had not used her real name for over a decade; I did not want to blow her cover.

Her response was emphatic: 'My real names, dear. Fezekile Ntsukela Kuzwayo.'

1

. . . .

Introduction

Jacob Zuma, the man who became the president of South Africa in 2009, was acquitted of rape in 2006. That is a legal truth. But what is the moral and ethical truth? Does the law go far enough in capturing the many truths that mark the journey of life?

I believe that the outcome of the Jacob Zuma rape trial was a triumph of law over justice. This is hardly a unique idea. The rape trial – and, indeed, Fezekile Kuzwayo's journey – presents us with an opportunity to interrogate concepts such as justice, equality and fairness, which the law may not always serve.

Fezekile Kuzwayo – or Fezeka, as she was also known – brought charges against African National Congress (ANC) deputy president Jacob Zuma for raping her at his home in Forest Town, Johannesburg, on the night of 2 November 2005. To protect her identity during the trial, she became known as Khwezi. Zuma argued that he had had consensual sex with Fezekile; his acquittal on 8 May 2006 is said to have helped clear his way to the presidency in 2009. Fezekile, an HIV-positive Aids activist, and her mother were hounded out of the country in the trial's aftermath. Her home was burnt down; to a chorus of calls to 'burn the bitch', she fled to Holland in 2006. Invoking widespread condemnation from medical professionals and Aids activists, among others, Zuma stated during the trial that he had taken a shower afterwards to reduce his risk of HIV infection.

Since the trial, I have thought about Khwezi all the time – followed her everywhere, and kept abreast of her activities. When she left South Africa, I wondered how I could have been a part of a society that had at worst allowed and at best observed her lynching. It was not enough that some of us spoke out – wrote columns, spoke on the radio, protested and tried to keep her memory alive long after she and her mother had left to settle in foreign lands, all because male power would not allow them to stay. We were still a part of a society that had allowed the erasure of a young woman's presence.

Life simply went on; the man at the centre of the storm became the president. It is surreal.

What did South Africa learn from the rape trial? Has society had the conversation about barriers to justice for women who approach the law? Have we fully confronted the entitlement of men in positions of power to young women's bodies – and how society facilitates this entitlement by not demanding the highest moral conduct from its men? Does the law, with its fixation on facts, represent the limits of human endeavour?

I have always imagined Khwezi's story as embodying Foucauldian discourse analysis of power relations. This is not a novel idea: gender researcher Nomboniso Gasa, author and academic Pumla Dineo Gqola, PhD fellow and gender relations expert Lisa Vetten, feminist and gender politics associate professor Sheila Meintjes, and author Mmatshilo Motsei have all written and spoken extensively about power relations in sexual violence in general, and in the Zuma rape trial in particular. Some, such as Gasa and Motsei, have gone further and reflected on the Jacob Zuma rape trial through the prism of culture and tradition.

Here, I add my voice – not for the first time – and venture into the subtleties and complexities of the Zuma/Khwezi power dynamic. The themes I explore are not new; I borrow extensively from feminist writers who have tackled them. But, to my knowledge, it is the first time that they are presented with an analysis of parts of the court record and a granular focus on some of the specific questions that were posed to Fezekile.

Feminist lawyers Sibongile Ndashe and Nikki Naylor have written and spoken extensively about legal instruments and courts as platforms of patriarchy. Furthermore, they have conceptualised the focus on Fezekile's sexual history during the trial as a form of victimisation. I move into this space precisely because the trial, and Fezekile's exercising her own agency by laying a charge, offered the nation an opportunity to engage with the complexities of gender-based violence and the power relations that determined the court's ruling. I contend that Fezekile stood no chance in a patriarchal trial.

It was Lucius Annaeus Seneca who said that 'we should always allow some time to elapse, for time discloses the truth'. Fezekile is gone, but the opportunity is ripe for us to revisit the trial and assess how it affected our lives and the frameworks it created for us, as a society, to have a meaningful and transformative conversation about sexual violence and the language of power.

In this book, Fezekile's voice rings loudly and defiantly. It is ironic, really, that I always knew where Fezekile was, but held back – I knew that many journalists had tried to speak to her, but that she had always run from them. First impressions last; had I pursued her aggressively, it would have put her off. I wanted her to know that I was writing, unapologetically, as a feminist who *believed* her – this being precisely why I approached her. We shared ideas and experiences. We spoke about our feelings; she poured her heart out to me, as she had done so many times to so many people. She cried, and laughed. She oscillated between hope and despair, joy and pain, laughter and tears. I have tried to capture this, her magnetic personality and her strength, and bring her back to life, however briefly. The rape trial may have been a significant chapter in her life, but it was not her entire life. She loved words. She loved to sing and dance, to talk, to read. She loved people.

I could never have anticipated her death, which has made this book very different from the one she and I discussed. I have filled the resulting gaps by speaking to her friends and extended family, people who knew her best and helped her in her darkest moments. Here, I visit her childhood through the friends and adults who raised her. More importantly – for Fezekile, at least – I try to tell the story of her father, Judson Kuzwayo. She feared that he would be forgotten, that many of his trusted comrades and friends would die before she could record their experiences of him. With her permission, I interviewed some of the people who shaped her life. Some declined, for different reasons, but many more were willing to speak.

At her funeral, I was convinced that the book had died with her, that I could claim no moral authority for writing her story now that she was no longer here to vouch for it. But being in Durban that day gave me the courage to carry on. Her friends from far afield – people who had supported her during the trial, who had helped her to leave South Africa and find safety after the trial, who had helped her to pick up the pieces and rebuild her life in Amsterdam, Tanzania and back in South Africa – rallied around this project and encouraged me to carry on. Yet this is neither an exhaustive nor an authoritative account of Fezekile's life.

Did Fezekile ever recover from her ordeal? What were her hopes and dreams? What had her life been like before that fateful night? Did she learn to laugh, sing and dance again, as she once had? In her darker moods, she would say, 'Today I am trying not to think at all. I am trying to crawl, and take things one fool at a time.' This was her mother's

Fezekile on a Dar es Salaam beach

favourite saying when human relationships overwhelmed her or became conflict-ridden. Yet in all our conversations, until the end, she spoke as someone who believed she could climb the mountains in her path.

But now Fezekile is dead. So many of her dreams will go unrealised. Her body returns to the soil, carrying all the hurts and disappointments of a life well lived, but not always on her terms. Her death, at the sunset of Jacob Zuma's presidency, feels like a scathing rebuke of the nation, a damning reminder of its complicity in her trauma and forced exile.

Khwezi *is* politics – a symbol of the arduous fight against political and patriarchal power, and against Zuma, its torchbearer. That she had to take on a different name, albeit a beautiful one lent to her by a friend, testifies to the physical and mental savagery inflicted upon her. But today, in these pages, she is here to reclaim her own name.

This is her story.

CHAPTER 1

'If you did not speak then, do not speak now'

'If you did not speak then, do not speak now. The feminists of South Africa are coming for you. Our rage cannot be stopped. Our rage is coming for you.'

Gender activist and One in Nine Campaign co-founder Dawn Cavanagh was furious. Those gathered at the Central City Methodist Church in Durban applauded her wildly. Cavanagh's words had opened a gaping wound, one that many women in South Africa feel. It is the wound caused by sexism, violence, poverty and discrimination.

South African women are, collectively, a pressure cooker waiting to explode. The rapes, the violence, the groping, the labels, the corrective rape and murder of lesbians and the abuse of children – it is debilitating. The fear is palpable, as is the determination not to cower and retreat. As women of South Africa, this is our home, too. Patriarchy cannot have the last word.

I looked around at this, the celebration of Fezekile's life. I hardly saw any of her father Judson's comrades – apart from Ivan Pillay, who had served under Judson in the MJK (Mandla Judson Kuzwayo) unit of Umkhonto we Sizwe (MK) in exile in late-1970s Swaziland. I had seen Pillay on the early-morning flight to Durban and had not realised, then, that he had been travelling to the funeral. It was particularly touching to have him there – only a few days earlier, charges relating to his tenure as deputy commissioner of the South African Revenue Service had been laid against him and finance minister Pravin Gordhan. Many believe the charges to have been trumped up, an attempt by Zuma to weaken his political opponents and pave the way for pliable officials to help him get his hand inside the cookie jar.

But this day was not about Zuma. It was Fezekile's farewell and, while I am loath to describe this sad day as beautiful, it was a beautiful send-off. We laughed as speakers reminded us of her idiosyncrasies; we smiled and felt strong when told about her courage, loyalty and zest for life. Her love for children was legendary. Teresa, with whom Fezekile stayed in Tanzania, gave a moving speech about her daughter, Zora, who has Down syndrome and to whom Fezekile used to demonstrate the utmost tenderness. She would play games with Zora without once looking at the time; when Zora entered the world of make-believe, Fezekile would happily enter this imaginary world with her. They would play for hours, talking to their imaginary friends, travelling to worlds where little girls were safe and happy. Perhaps these games were as much for Fezekile as they were for Zora.

Shaun Mellors, a South African based in London who works for the International HIV/AIDS Alliance, had been Fezekile's mentor. He had been instrumental in mobilising the networks that had created a home for Fezekile and her mother Beauty in Amsterdam. He gave a gentle, beautiful tribute to his friend, then lambasted those who had abandoned her. He had harsh words for those who were trying to own her now, asking, 'Where were they when Fez was desperate? Where were they when her pain kept her awake at night? Where were they when she had nothing?'

Prudence Mabele, founder of the Positive Women's Network, an advocacy group for women living with HIV/Aids, said in a voice that carried the authority that can only be commanded by one who is comfortable in her own skin: 'Zuma will *never* be my president!' She sang and danced, amplifying her voice when those of the mourners dulled, and sat with teary-eyed Shaun, comforting him. With Shaun and Dawn Cavanagh, she had formed a triumvirate dedicated to Fezekile's protection.

Briefly, in the outpouring of love for Fezekile, I forgot how we had struggled to find a venue for her funeral service. It was quite bizarre that, all week, Fezekile's family had battled, and that the Methodist Church in KwaMashu had suddenly become unavailable.

Two days before the funeral, on Thursday 13 October, I had been roped in to help find a church. Auntie Bunie (Bunie Sexwale, a gender and anti-apartheid activist who was very close to Fezekile) had sent me an SMS explaining the family's predicament and saying that she was flying to Durban and had contacted everyone who may have been able to help in the hope that something would come up. I hate asking for favours – it brings me great discomfort. But deep down, I think I wanted to demonstrate that I was not just interested in Fezekile as a subject, but that I had grown to love her. I braced myself by pouring a glass of wine, and resolved to start making calls.

It did not occur to me to call my industrious and conscientious friend Mark Heywood of the Treatment Action Campaign (TAC). The TAC fights to provide life-saving, affordable antiretrovirals (ARVs) to HIV-positive South Africans. Mark's bona fides as a committed and fearless activist are indisputable, and his activism and commitment to social justice initiatives in South Africa are unparalleled. He goes to South Africa's neglected corners, where he rolls up his sleeves and speaks to the poor while exposing the corruption that continues to impoverish many South Africans and deny them their rights. More recently, he has faced the might of the state and, despite intimidation and threats, been the leading voice in the #SaveSouthAfrica and #ZumaMustFall marches that have swept through South Africa.

At that very moment, he sent me a text message: 'Khwezi's death made me think of you. I hope you are okay. It is so tragic and all so wrong.'

Without asking for help, I messaged back that a local church had just cancelled on the family.

He responded simply: 'Do you need help?'

'I do, desperately. Anywhere in Durban would work.'

'On it, will make some calls now.'

Despite his being in Geneva, within ten minutes he had not only made contact with someone who could help, but that person – Debbie Matthews – had already phoned around. Debbie was a contact of his from the civil society networks in Durban. Incidentally, Debbie and Fezekile had worked together on HIV/Aids initiatives in the late 1990s.

Debbie saved the day. Reverend Akhona Gxamza of Durban's Central City Methodist Church graciously agreed to allow the service to take place there, even though Fezekile had not been a member of his congregation.

I sent a message to Debbie: 'I do not know how to thank you for this generous gift to Fezeka. If no one has thanked you, I want to say a big THANK YOU. I am arriving at 9 a.m. tomorrow and if you are there, I'd like to meet you and give you a big hug.'

Her response was a sign that life and the universe work in mysterious ways: 'Pleasure, Redi. I will be there. I first met Fezeka and her mother in 1995. The church is an inner-city mission church so the premises are a bit run down but it has a long history of serving and being a gathering place for the oppressed, dispossessed and abused. This resonates with the causes and struggles that Khwezi stood for during her life.'

The venue was only secured at about 9 p.m. on that Thursday. Half an hour later, the ANC released a statement announcing the Hands Off Zuma rally. It was to start right next to the church at the same time as

11

Fezekile's funeral service. The marchers promised to bring Durban to a standstill with song and dance. About fifteen thousand were expected; roads would be closed.

Even in death, Fezekile had to face one last fight.

Some in the organising team began to panic. I did, too. But my anxiety lasted for no more than five minutes. I began to laugh: Zuma's supporters would be late. They were always late. By the time they flooded the CBD, we'd be long gone and Fezekile would be resting, safely, in her grave, her new home.

I was right. A handful of ANC supporters made some noise during the service, but nothing more. On the evening news, it was clear that thousands of Zuma supporters had, indeed, turned up for the march. But Fezekile was resting at last by this time.

Perhaps the march had been organised to mitigate the sting of what was expected to be a scathing report on state capture in South Africa. The outgoing Public Protector, Thuli Madonsela, was scheduled to release her state capture report the day before the funeral. In the South African lexicon, state capture had become synonymous with the Zuma presidency. It referred to a few individuals' attempt to control state coffers and tenders – prominent among them the Gupta family, personal friends of Zuma and business partners of Zuma's son Duduzane. Some Cabinet ministers and former civil servants (although very few) had come forward to expose how the Gupta family had approached them, offering them money and senior government positions in exchange for their making decisions that would enrich Gupta-owned companies.

The country was outraged. In anticipation of the report pointing the finger at Zuma, the ANC in KwaZulu-Natal decided, at the eleventh hour, to stage the bold rally in the province where Zuma's support was strongest.

Returning home that afternoon, my eyes swollen from crying and the adrenalin wearing off after the anxiety, early morning and logistics, I

Fezekile's casket at her funeral service at Durban's
Central City Methodist Church

recalled a late-night conversation in which I had asked Fezekile if she had come to terms with everything that had happened to her.

She paused for a long time. Then asked, 'How do you define "come to terms"?'

'I don't know. You know, like losing a limb, your eyesight. Something you cannot reverse. You wake up with it every day but are not always conscious of it? You accept it as part of your life, a chapter in your journey. Something like that.'

'I wish I had lost a limb. Rape is like death.'

I thought about saying it, but did not: *But you did not die, Fez. They didn't destroy you.*

13

CHAPTER 2

A young life in exile

'It's life. It's cruel that way. You start a journey. You don't complete it. It completes you, it decides when you must get off.'

This was Fezekile being philosophical about her father's death, but I know that the event had marked her in a profound way. She felt that her journey in life would not be complete without an effort to document her father's. She was obsessed with the idea; every time she thought she would start, life interrupted her.

Fezekile's biggest fear was that her father would be forgotten. She wanted it recorded that Diza, as he was known by those close to him, had been a principled, gallant soldier, a loving father who had lifted her up to the skies and tickled her until she had broken into a sweat and lost her voice from laughing so hard.

She told me that he was larger than life. Most children think this, so I set about testing it for myself.

Judson Kuzwayo was born in Natal, the same province as Jacob Zuma. He joined the ANC when he was just sixteeen years old. His education was interrupted when he attempted to leave the country illegally for military training. He went on to become a senior commander of MK, the ANC's military wing. So prominent was he that a unit, the

Judson Kuzwayo during his time as a
senior MK leader in Swaziland

MJK unit, was named after him. Zuma led this unit.

Like Zuma – and at the same time as Zuma – he was given a ten-year sentence on Robben Island in 1963. This prison housed the man who was, perhaps, the most famous prisoner of the twentieth century, Nobel laureate and first democratically elected president of South Africa Nelson Mandela, along with his equally famous and revered comrades Walter Sisulu, Govan Mbeki, Ahmed Kathrada, Andrew Mlangeni, Elias Motsoaledi and many other luminaries of the struggle.

Like many comrades who were incarcerated for a long period, he pursued his education and obtained his matric qualification. He loved to read and was interested in issues of inequality, racism and human

15

Judson and Beauty Kuzwayo on their wedding day in KwaMashu,
flanked by family and friends

Little Fezekile in KwaMashu during the 1970s, before the family went into exile

rights. It was no surprise that, when he was released from prison, he was drawn to academic life; he worked as a researcher at the erstwhile University of Natal's sociology department. During this time, he kept his feet firmly in the liberation movement and remained involved in its activities – he assisted Mac Maharaj to escape from South Africa in 1977, for example. Later, he was to become an ANC commander in Swaziland.

Prison had done nothing to quell his activism and militancy: in the 1970s, he was constantly under surveillance, and in and out of jail. There were many Christmases spent behind bars, away from Beauty, his young wife, who was pregnant in 1974 and 1975. Between 1975 and 1977, Beauty was often alone with baby Fezekile; Judson would be detained for months on end, then released, only to be rearrested. He eventually left the country in July 1977, a month before Fezekile's second birthday. The family moved to Swaziland, where Judson was

17

Former minister of justice and ANC underground operative Penuell Maduna,

who served with Judson Kuzwayo in Mozambique and Harare,

speaking at Judson's funeral in Harare, May 1985

stationed until 1983. He was appointed the ANC's chief representative in Lesotho and, a year later, transferred to Zimbabwe.

In May 1985, three months before his forty-fourth birthday, Judson died in a car accident in Harare. Fezekile was almost ten years old. Although she remained convinced that foul play had been involved, all of Judson's comrades with whom I spoke believed it was genuinely a tragic accident.

It is a mark of Judson's prominence and seniority that Robert Mugabe, the lifetime president of Zimbabwe who was prime minister at the time, sent a personal and heartfelt message to ANC president Oliver Tambo upon his passing.

ANC veteran Alfred Nzo (centre), the longest-serving secretary general of the ANC
and the democratic South Africa's first minister of foreign affairs,
at Judson Kuzwayo's funeral

In reply, Tambo wrote that 'Comrade Kuzwayo has joined the martyrs of our struggle, who, by their selfless dedication and sacrifice, have promoted our struggle to new heights and inspired us to greater efforts to bring about a speedy triumph of our cause. The work he has done in soldering the relations between our respective parties and people will remain a shining beacon to his memory'.[1]

But life had other ideas: Comrade Zuma appropriated the body of Comrade Kuzwayo's daughter, her house was burnt down, and she was forced into a second exile, far from the land whose liberation was Judson's sole purpose.

Many of Judson's comrades survived the brutal war against apartheid

Fezekile (right) and her elder half-sister Zintle (left)
at their father's funeral

and went on to take up prominent positions in the country's democratic civil service. Members of the MJK unit included Jayendra Naidoo, and Yunis and Moe Shaik – brothers who had given their all to the struggle against apartheid and had earned their dues as worthy operatives, but, sadly, became known by the larger South African public for their relationship to their younger brother Schabir, who became Zuma's financial adviser. In 2005, Judge Hilary Squires found Shaik guilty of corruption (for paying Zuma R1.2 million and soliciting a bribe from French arms company Thomson-CSF) and fraud (for writing off more than R1 million of Zuma's debts).[2] Bizarrely, Zuma was not charged for this corrupt

Beauty (in black) at her husband's funeral, flanked by ANC comrades, with little
Fezekile looking on as the ground swallows her father's coffin

relationship. But the other Shaik brothers, Yunis and Moe, earned their stripes as underground operatives working with, and sometimes reporting to, Zuma.

Fezekile did not remember the first two years of her life in South Africa. For all intents and purposes, her childhood began and ended in exile. Her father, she said, told her a lot of stories about Robben Island, including his time spent sharing a cell with his comrades, including Zuma. It is worth reflecting on what this means. What happens when people are jailed together, spending every minute of every day together – for ten years? Does a brotherhood not develop? Does a solid bond built

21

on sweat, pain and sacrifice not grow? Do they not spend hours talk-ing about the cause that has sent them to this wretched prison? Share their fears and hopes? Establish an intimate knowledge of one another's strengths and weaknesses? Become brothers? Ten years in jail together, and many more years out of prison, fighting the same cause. What do we call that bond? What does it take to destroy it?

Initially, I could not speak to Beauty, Fezekile's mother. She had, according to Fezekile, 'started losing her mind, losing her words'. But I wanted to know how Beauty coped – a young wife with a small baby and a husband who was in and out of prison, the family's safety not guaranteed.

'How did she feel about that?'

'*Dade* (sister), did anyone ask women how they felt? They just got on with life.'

And, 'My life was built on love, you know, uncles, aunties, their chil-dren who became sisters, you know. All built on love.'

I am not convinced that this is true. Fezekile was adrift, always searching and seeking a place to claim as her own, a place where her heart was safe. Her mother also left her at some stage when they were living in Zimbabwe. Beauty was a dancer and actress, and would go on regular tours with the famous musical *Ipi Tombi* (after the isiZulu '*iphi intombi*', meaning 'where is the girl?'). Her career took her as far afield as Russia. For some time, little Fezeka remained in Zimbabwe, being raised by aunties and uncles of the struggle.

I became familiar with Fezekile's proclivity for romance, her desire to make beautiful and mystical that which is ordinary. She felt deeply and had words to describe, quite richly, everything she thought and felt. Her diary entries, long before the trial, showed a Fezekile who constantly imagined what her life would have been like had her father been alive. She conceded that her preoccupation with her father had held her back for twenty years. She described her father as someone who gave her a normal and therefore 'wonderful childhood in abnormal situations'. And then she wrote that he was a wonderful husband, something which she knew not to be entirely true, given Judson's indiscretions. But he was still her father and children love their parents, even when they cheat.

This heroic narrative of her father did not end, even when she chastised him for some of his flaws. A few weeks before the trial, when she was alone in witness protection, she wrote in her diary: 'The other day, I had a big missing Daddy moment, wishing he was here, that he had never left. Yet, in reality, he cannot come back.'

Years later, she would reflect deeply on her longing for her father and see it as the main reason she had sought Zuma out. 'Maybe if I was not missing Daddy so much, if I was not so hungry for stories about him, I would not have allowed myself to get closer to Zuma and, you know, it, it would not have happened.'

In another diary entry, Fezekile uses her experience at the hands of males to question how her own father may have turned out had he stayed alive. She wonders whether he, too, would have turned out the way 'so many uncles turned out'. In conversations with her therapist Kevin, and her close friend, Hlabi Msibi-Gordon, whom she regarded as a sister, she becomes philosophical: 'Better, perhaps, that they are gone, and will always remain heroes in our eyes and in our hearts. And heroes they are.'

But, in pages of her diary that follow this one, Fezekile seems to entertain a more realistic assessment of her father and his fallibility. She writes him a letter:

> Daddy, in your life and your death, our relationship has grown, transformed and been bad and good. We have drifted apart and I have had issues with you that mostly were really none of my

business. As Mama Samkele said, she realised the futility of having issues with the dead. Kimmy helped me to work through the issues I had, specifically with you cheating on Mama. I don't mean it in a bad way towards Sesi and Zintle [Fezekile's half-siblings] but actually, unlike them, you never did cheat on me or not spend time with me. I've also had times when I blame you for things that have happened in my life, bad things that I feel you would have protected me from had you been here.

The heroic narrative returns in the second half of the letter:

But really, perhaps you would have protected me too much had you been around. Now I feel grateful for the times we had together, and also lucky when I see people whose fathers are alive but might as well be dead. Actually, some people wish that their fathers were dead. So I have come full circle. You are dead and that's it. I should focus my energy on holding on to the memories of the nine years and eight months we had and stop trying to find you in other people or making them you.

In trying to find solace and closure about her father's absence, she had a moment of powerful realisation: 'You know, maybe it is good that my father died young. I had this conversation with Hlabi and Kimmy about our fathers.'

Hlabi and Kimmy's father was Mandla Blackman Msibi, a senior MK operative who died in Swaziland. He had been close to Judson, and their wives had been friends; it was only natural that the children would also have formed their own special bond.

Kimmy and Fezekile had a deep connection, regarding each other as sisters. Their mothers, coincidentally, were both known as Beauty.

Beauty was Fezekile's mother's real name, and Kimmy's mother's was Betty. But, because of the dangers of the anti-apartheid struggle and the need to be incognito, Betty had adopted the alias Beauty. When the two families became close, Fezekile's mother became known as big Beauty, being older, and Kimmy's mother, small Beauty.

When we spoke about the father theme, Fezekile had just returned from the unveiling of Mandla's tombstone in Manzini. It was April 2016. She was animated and happy, pleased to have re-established connections with her exile family. Stories of fallen comrades, even so many years after the trial, always made her feel close to her own father.

She told me that 'Uncle Siphiwe' (Siphiwe Nyanda) had spoken at the unveiling, and said that Msibi would have been proud of the ANC's achievements, yet saddened by some developments. Nyanda is a decorated former MK commander, and former chief of the South African National Defence Force (SANDF) and minister of communications. He is known for his daring confrontation with apartheid forces who had infiltrated the house in which he and some comrades were staying in Mozambique. In the ambush, there had been gunshots and many casualties. But Nyanda had escaped, going on to become one of Zuma's staunchest supporters in the government of the democratic South Africa. He is now a fierce critic of corruption and state capture.

Zuma did not attend the unveiling, even though Msibi had served under him and been his contemporary. There was a mere handful of people at the unveiling, Beauty among them, as well as Thenjiwe Mtintso, a luminary and one of the most prominent female figures of the liberation. Many of the comrades with whom Msibi had served were not there.

Mandla Msibi died of a heart attack at the age of 37 while on a mission to Swaziland in 1980.

Fezekile felt that the unveiling had been 'healing for me and Ma.

You know, being there, among people who have loved us and love us to this day'. She had been reminded, at the unveiling, of a conversation she'd had with Kimmy and Hlabi shortly after laying the rape charge against Zuma. In it, Hlabi had told Fezekile that, 'Our fathers can't fail any more. They are not alive to mess up their legacy. They will always be good in our eyes. They died heroes and that cannot be changed.'

'Why do you think that would have changed had they stayed alive?' I asked.

'Well, Hlabi and I had discussed, back in the day, at the start of the trial, that with Malume [Uncle] Zuma doing this, we can never know what [our fathers] might have turned out to be like. We are glad they are dead, if you know what I mean.'

'Mmm … and I notice you referred to him as Malume Zuma.'

She did not respond.

· · ·

I sit down to speak to Ivan Pillay, the former deputy commissioner of the South African Revenue Service, whom I'd seen at the funeral. Everyone who had been connected to Judson Kuzwayo's MK history had led me to Pillay. Moe Shaik had said to me, 'You will not find a nicer, more decent human being than Ivan.'

Fezekile loved Malume Ivan. She'd said, 'He is just one of those people who bothered about Ma and me. Who did not leave us. He restores my faith in men.'

Indeed, Ivan did not leave them. When the exiles returned, years after Judson had died, Ivan stayed in touch with Beauty and Fezekile. In about 2003, he invited Fezekile to lunch at a Pretoria restaurant.

He had not seen her in many years. When they saw each other, Fezekile ran up to him and picked him up.

'At this stage, she had grown quite big, you know,' he says, before bursting into laughter. He laughs so hard that it is clear he did not mind his late comrade's daughter lifting him up in full view of other patrons in the restaurant. 'Fezeka literally lifted me off my feet, right there at the restaurant.'

Ivan is a lean man, so Fezekile could not have struggled to lift him up.

He had not recovered from Fezekile's telling him that she was HIV-positive. At the restaurant, she was loud and happy. Ivan uses the word 'exuberant' to describe her mood that day.

After Fezekile's death, Ivan visited Auntie Bunie's home to pay his respects. He found Beauty a sorry sight: 'No tears, no emotions. It was like she was not aware that she had just lost her daughter.'

Ivan had been very close to Judson. Fezekile held on to those relationships; I guess it was a way of keeping her father alive. Like everyone with whom I spoke, Ivan believes Judson's death was a tragic accident.

Ivan, Judson and Shadrack Maphumulo were the comrades who had set up the political unit within MK. At that time, MK had started sending cadres for military training. But it was thought that military action without a political strategy was doomed to fail. Politics had to guide military action so that the ideology and cause for which MK was fighting would endure long after arms had been laid down. Combatants had to appreciate that theirs was not just an exercise of brawn, but an insightful grasp of the ideology for which they were fighting – otherwise, Ivan says, 'the struggle would be reduced to nothing more than petrol bombs, guns and camouflage'.

'The lack of a sound political foundation resulted in so many casualties,' he reflects. 'We lost a lot of guys, good guys, because of a lack of vison and direction.'

Judson had been excellent at identifying and recruiting operatives, Ivan notes: 'His pleasant, firm and quiet manner made him a great recruiter.'

Ivan remembers Judson as a very neat gentleman. Often, they would have meetings in his bedroom. While other comrades would sit on the bed discussing politics or just having a laugh, Judson would be ironing his shirts and pants.

'He was so meticulous. He would not stop until there was that line running along the middle, the length of his pants. *Motshetshe.* We call it *motshetshe* and all black men want that.'

Judson was a terrible driver, and only learnt to drive in his forties. So bad was he that he got into an accident right inside the yard of the house at which he was staying in Swaziland, where it should have been easiest to manoeuvre. He hit the wall; there was extensive damage to the car. At the time, the ANC had very strict lines of authority and an exhausting bureaucracy. In keeping with the ANC's abiding love for reports, Judson was required to write a report about the incident. According to Mac Maharaj, Judson had written that 'the wall came fast and drove straight into me'. This is how that incident was recorded.

Judson loved his family and was very close to his children. 'But he had problems with women.'

'What kind of problems?'

Ivan blushes, and cannot bring himself to say the words.

'You know, had trouble in that area and it used to upset Beauty.' Ivan has a devilish smile on his face so I get what he means by 'problem'.

'Oh, he was a ladies' man, so *he* was the problem,' I challenge him.

'*Ja*, and Beauty got into some unpleasant fights.'

And then something happened that Ivan cannot explain. Ivan was infiltrated into South Africa for a few months and, when he returned to

Swaziland, Judson had been moved to Zimbabwe.

'It was a very confusing time. The move did not really make sense because the unit needed Judson's presence and there was no proper, or effective, handover. There was no clear communication, but a decision had been made to send Judson to Zimbabwe.'

The move weakened the unit. But it was in the ANC's DNA, even in exile – perhaps especially in exile – that cadres should toe the party line; asking too many questions could have jeopardised their safety. Ivan and the rest of the team had to trust that there was a compelling reason for Judson to be moved.

'I never saw Judson ever again,' Ivan says.

Ivan had heard through the ANC grapevine that something had happened to Fezekile when she was a child. I let him share details before confirming them, and he is spot on about the dates.

'I heard about some incidents in her childhood, I think she was five, and again at twelve?'

He is correct. She was five, twelve and thirteen.

'How did you know about it?'

'It was spoken about and some comrades knew I had been close to her father so the news reached me. But it is an indictment of our movement that it did not deal decisively with such incidents.'

'So, it was covered up?'

'That is another way of looking at it. And perhaps typical of organisations that depend on secrecy and closing ranks.'

. . .

Zintle, Fezekile's half-sister, pretty much confirms that their father had had multiple relationships in exile and fathered a couple of children.

Zintle is Judson's eldest daughter. Fezekile is next in age; the rest are younger than Fezekile, born after Judson married Beauty.

'Who knows – there could be others,' Zintle laughs.

She is a defence force nurse at the Union Buildings, known by her colleagues as Doctor Nurse. A meticulous nurse, she is also known for being the comedian at work. At the entrance to the canteen, everyone knows her, laughs at her constant jokes and accepts the nicknames that she gives everyone she encounters. She is also a trained sangoma (traditional healer) and an artist who is busy with an art course. She tells me she is also taking a course in body healing. This part of her reminds me of Fezekile: always restless, always searching, always moving.

There does not seem to have been any love lost between Fezekile and Zintle. When I asked Fezekile whether she had any siblings, she gave me an emphatic no. I knew this not to be true. But before I could challenge her, she added, 'It's a bit complicated. Biological, yes, but not in the way siblings should be siblings.'

There was a time when Zintle and Fezekile had been estranged, but Fezekile had been close to Zintle's daughter Nokuzola.

Zintle tells me that Nokuzola had simply adored Fezekile, and called her 'mother'. Some of Fezekile's friends in South Africa, Tanzania and the Netherlands have met Nokuzola and testify to the mother–daughter bond, even though Fezekile was no more than ten years older than Nokuzola. On the evening that Fezekile ended up at Zuma's house, she had planned to travel to Swaziland to visit 'her daughter' Nokuzola, whose young child had been bitten by a snake. Fezekile had been agitated and determined to go to Swaziland when, she alleges, Zuma dissuaded her from travelling. This matter was discussed extensively at the trial.

Nokuzola and Zintle had their own disagreements; Nokuzola went to live with her aunt Fezekile and her step-grandmother for a while. But mother and daughter patched things up. At the time of Fezekile's death, Nokuzola was back in her mother's fold.

'Why were you and Fez not close?' I ask Zintle.

'It's a long story. I had no problem with Fezeka, but Beauty and I had strained relations throughout, and that limited my interaction with, and access to, Fezeka.'

At this point, I want to ask her about an incident that Ivan Pillay had shared with me. While I am still formulating the words, she boldly delves into that history. According to Zintle, Beauty would not accept her. It did not help that Zintle was the spitting image of Judson: everyone who visited their home in Swaziland marvelled at the resemblance. Zintle's own mother had abandoned her, leaving her with her aunt to go off and marry another man. Judson was in jail, and could not take care of his daughter.

Zintle was 'sold' by this aunt to another family in Bizana, a small village on the border between KwaZulu-Natal and the Eastern Cape.

'They treated me very well. I felt loved, I had food to eat and lacked for nothing.'

Though that family did not treat her like someone whom they had 'bought', it must have stung to be abandoned by her own family, her father banished to an island prison.

When Judson was released from prison, he searched for his daughter and demanded custody of her. For the second time in her life as a little girl, Zintle was uprooted.

'How do you feel about your father, who had all these risky political activities, coming out of prison and searching for you? He was obviously a responsible father?'

'Oh, is that how you see it? All children need is love, regardless of who gives it. He took me away from a loving family, to a life of suffering.'

31

Zintle joined Judson, Beauty and baby Fezekile in Swaziland. She arrived to a well-established family of father, stepmother and half-sister, the outsider who had to fit in. The domestic situation was turbulent: Judson and Beauty clashed bitterly over Zintle. According to Zintle, Judson would walk away while Zintle was given what she regards as unfair hidings. Zintle says her father did not protect her at all. Instead, he would storm off to one of his lady friends. I am not sure how Zintle knew, as a child, that Judson was storming off to a lover, but I let it go. Beauty felt that Zintle had been imposed on her, and that she'd had no say in the decision to bring her to Swaziland. Judson, on the other hand, would part with neither his child nor his wife. It was a recipe for disaster.

Judson became so miserable that he apparently attempted suicide. Zintle says he tried to hang himself; his comrade and senior, Moses Mabhida, had walked in just as he was about to kick the chair. Zintle must have been in her teens by then – old enough to understand what was going on around her – but I wonder how she knows with certainty that Judson's suicide attempt was sparked by an unhappy marriage and that she was the cause of the unhappiness. At this point, Judson had other children and, the exile community being a small world, Beauty knew about them. The infidelity must have taken a toll on their marriage and Beauty's emotional health.

Coupled with this, Beauty had three miscarriages between 1978 and 1981: one at eight weeks, another at twelve weeks, and the third – particularly hard – at an advanced stage of the pregnancy. According to Fezekile, she had felt the baby kick but, at four months, life had left her womb.

She was confounded with pain. This was Beauty's state of mind when Judson brought Zintle to live with them.

Matters between Beauty and Zintle came to a head when, after a lot of shouting between Beauty and Judson, Beauty walked into the bathroom as Zintle was preparing to take a bath. She had a big knife in her hand and was coming straight for Zintle. Zintle truly believes that Beauty was going to stab her. She screamed, ducking and running around the room before managing to access the door. Judson was in another room, quiet, making no attempt to intervene.

With the help of some comrades, Zintle was removed from her family and taken to Mozambique. From then on, she did not interact much with them, but saw her father when he travelled to Maputo and, later, Tanzania and Zimbabwe. Zintle would go on to live and complete her nursing education in Tanzania. This is where she was when she received the news that her father had died in a car accident. At that time, she says, Fezekile was living in Zimbabwe and Beauty was in Russia to pursue her dance training. I am trying to process how it must have been for ten-year-old Fezekile to be alone, reliant on the love and affection of the exiled aunts and uncles, when her father died. Who broke the news to her? Who held her? Who told her it would all be all right?

Zintle and her stepmother had, and still have, a strange relationship. At some times in their lives after Judson had died, they seemed to smoke the peace pipe, calling each other and exchanging pleasantries. But sometimes, a cold war of sorts would break out between them. When it did, it affected Zintle's relationship with her half-sister.

There would be more conflict between Beauty and Fezekile on the one side and Zintle and their paternal aunt, Judson's sister Cordelia, on the other. Judson's ancestral home was a vast piece of land. In keeping with the laws of traditional leadership and collective ownership, they lived on the land – it was allocated to the Kuzwayos, but under the stewardship of the local chief. This is a complex arrangement that denies families agency and authority over their land. If the chief is corrupt, it is easy for the powerful members of the village to buy his favour and secure more land, dispossessing the vulnerable. Those in favour of this hierarchical style of land ownership argue that it instils collective responsibility and shared values, and ensures that outsiders cannot usurp the community's authority.

The Kuzwayos 'owned' property and land under this arrangement. It seems that, through her marriage to Judson, Beauty owned a part of the property, consisting of rondavels. Even before their second exile, the property had been neglected. It fell into even deeper neglect after Beauty and Fezekile had left for Amsterdam: the structures were vandalised and the property became so dilapidated that it looked like a ghost town. According to Zintle, heinous crimes were committed there – it was isolated, and the grass and trees had grown to such heights as to conceal the presence of any human activity. Zintle says women were raped there, drugs were exchanged, and some people were murdered on the spot.

She says Beauty's in-laws decided to intervene and take charge of the property. They also received notice from the traditional authorities that unless they rehabilitated the land and property, it would fall wholly under the chief's authority and be allocated to someone else.

Zintle says that her aunt and her son decided to rescue the property to keep it in the family's name. They cleaned it up, but it had amassed arrears in rates and taxes. By the time Beauty returned from her second exile, the electricity and water had been cut off. She went to the local municipality to resolve the issue and found that the property had been registered in her nephew's name, the son of Judson's sister. Zintle and her aunt insist that they had not hijacked the property, but had registered it in the nephew's name to keep it in the family. Beauty felt that this was an act of aggression and collusion on the part of her in-laws, and believed that they had stolen her land.

By the time Fezekile died, many of these feuds had not been resolved.

The disagreements and differences extended to the rituals of her funeral, and the roles that different people in her life should play. Her father's family had strong beliefs about how her soul should be transported to the other side and how her body should be prepared for burial. Some in her extended 'family' of friends and activists also insisted that the Fezekile they knew had held certain beliefs that had to be respected and reflected in her final journey.

One major disagreement was about how Fezekile's body should be dressed. Fezekile loved being in the nude, and walking around the house in her birthday suit. The family was informed that this is how she would like to depart, and that nobody should dress her body. This is an area of contestation: another version is that close friends had tried to go to the funeral parlour to prepare her body for the journey back to KwaZulu-Natal, but that, in a comedy of errors, their car had been broken into and the bag with her clothes stolen. Zintle was also told that the car had broken down on the way to the funeral home.

This was communicated to the family as a sign that Fezekile did not want to be clothed on her final journey. Both Judson's and Beauty's side of the family were appalled at the idea: the dressing of the body was a sacred task for members of the family.

'Many people played a role in Fezeka's life and we are grateful, but they did not know when to step back,' Zintle says. 'Fezeka had been denied her dignity in life and it was cruel to deprive her of her dignity in death. To be naked in a casket and be viewed by everyone just seemed wrong. Also, at a time like this, the family must be given space to perform its rituals and observe its own dictates.'

. . .

Ebrahim Ebrahim is a struggle veteran who served a fifteen-year sentence, which started in 1964, on Robben Island. He was in prison at the same time as Zuma and Judson. He worked with Judson in Swaziland in the late 1970s and early 1980s. Like so many, he paid dearly for his involvement with the banned ANC and MK. In Swaziland, he was abducted and sent to South Africa to face treason charges. During his incarceration, he was tortured in the most brutal way.

Ebrahim is also known as a staunch Zuma supporter, but as Moe Shaik tells me, 'Yes, he is very close to the president, but not uncritical.'

Ebrahim does not remember the circumstances that led to Judson ending up on Robben Island: 'There were so many of us. We had a common cause and did not ask each other too many questions. It was a security risk, you see.'

But he does know that Judson was very disciplined and 'committed to the struggle': 'He was one of those comrades who always played by the rules,' he says. 'No matter what. I remember that he was hardworking and disciplined and always particular about implementing ANC policy.'

Fezekile would be extremely proud of this.

I speak to Ebrahim after Fezekile's death. She would have been delighted to hear how, according to Ebrahim, Judson used to carry pictures of Beauty.

'He was very proud when he showed us pictures of her performing in a Shakespearean play,' Ebrahim recalls. 'Yes, I remember that. He was so happy that she was acting in that play. Oh, and we had a choir on Robben Island,' he continues. 'Judson sang in the choir. He was quite a chorister.'

I wonder whether Fezekile knew this. It would have pleased her greatly, as she sang in a choir herself and always looked forward to performances.

. . .

Fezekile had, I believe, trained her mind to remember exile charitably and with nostalgia. She spoke lovingly of her childhood friends, singing and dancing, and just being little girls. She remembered home-cooked meals and little treats, like canned peaches and candied apples. She told me that she did not honestly enjoy some of these treats, but that they were colourful and 'beautifully put together' – that she had to eat them and pretend they were delicious.

She remembered uncles who used to send them on errands, pick them up, tickle them and give them treats. She remembered the love, the warmth and the men and women who cared. She remembered them all. She remembered Uncle Ronnie (Kasrils), Uncle Dumisani (Nduli), Uncle Ivan (Pillay).

She remembered Uncle Zuma, and hoped that he would help her to write a book about her father, since he had so many stories about him, and spoke of him not only as a comrade and friend, but as a brother.

She also remembered the three events in exile – occurring when she was five, twelve and thirteen – that changed her life forever.

. . .

'Do you know who had done it?' Adv Kemp J Kemp, Jacob Gedleyihlekisa Zuma's counsel, asked Fezekile in the Johannesburg High Court.[3]

Yes, she knew. Everybody knew. There had been no justice for her then, either.

When she was five years old, living in Swaziland, she went next door to an aunt's home to run a bath. For many, exile was about communal living and sharing. Even as an adult, Fezekile lived this way. She

37

welcomed everyone into her home; in turn, she believed she could find a home in those of others.

It had not crossed little Fez's mind that going over to Auntie Martha's – who lived with her brother, a man in his early thirties – would pose any danger to her. Fezekile wrote in her diary – and it is on the court record – that the uncle ran a bath for her and instructed her to take off her clothes. He then took her into his bedroom and raped her.

The uncles, who were principled enough to fight a noble fight against an oppressive, racist system, lacked the morality to appreciate the gravity of their violation of a little girl. To fight an evil system, surely one must have a sense of justice? Not when it comes to women and children's bodies. The war against apartheid, fought across women's bodies on different fronts. Fezekile should have been safe in this small world called exile, populated, ostensibly, by those who had a common cause and were one another's family. Fezekile's story is their story.

Seven years later, twelve-year-old Fezekile had lost her beloved father. She described to me how distraught she still was, and how she longed for his protective presence. Uncles who showed love and affection for her made a huge impression on her. In a diary entry, Fezekile wrote: 'As always when mama left the bed early, I went to Malume Godfrey's bed. I have always been scared of sleeping alone, I am not sure really, just as far back as I can remember I have never liked sleeping alone, always loved cuddling up to someone'.

For Fezekile, there was nothing odd about a young girl getting into bed with a close uncle, especially with her mother there: 'On the side was a chair that my mother sat on in the morning when I and Uncle Godfrey were sleeping,' she said to me. 'Ma would always wake up early, leaving me alone in bed, and then I would go to Uncle Godfrey's bed and sleep or just lie in it with him while mama did some housework.

Sometimes she would come in and sit on the chair and the three of us would chat for a while.'

This speaks to a relationship of trust and openness. Perhaps what is odd here is not a little girl getting into bed with an uncle, in front of her mother, but that the uncle and society interpret this as an invitation for 'consensual' sex. It is also worth noting that Fezekile considered Godfrey to be an uncle, albeit one much younger than her late father. In writing about this incident in her diary, long before the Zuma matter, she refers to Godfrey as 'Uncle'.

On one particular day, when Beauty had left earlier than usual to go to the ANC offices, she did what she always did: she slipped out of her bed and got into Uncle Godfrey's, curling up, facing away from him, and falling back into a deep sleep. What the court heard during Zuma's rape trial was: 'I really cannot say how long it was or how he started, all I remember was that I was half asleep and as I was trying to wake up myself he was undressing me and the time I was awake enough to figure out what was happening he was on top of me and my underwear was coming off. He lodged his penis into my vagina and started thrusting.'

At age thirteen, Fezekile says she was virtually kidnapped, bundled into a car and taken to the house of a grown man called Mashaya. He raped her there. Godfrey's girlfriend found her in Mashaya's house. She beat Fezekile severely, because she had stayed in the house. In this sorry saga involving two grown men and a thirteen-year-old girl, the adult girlfriend of one of the men saw fit to hit the thirteen-year-old.

As Fezekile once told me, had it been her mother who died in exile, her life may have turned out differently. The struggle, she said, was much friendlier towards, and accommodating of, men.

'But surely not, Fez? There are so many females who have made their mark in a democratic South Africa?'

She wasn't convinced, and believed strongly that those who had made

39

Fezekile as a little girl growing up in Swaziland

a mark were married to male activists or were connected, somehow, to strong and authoritative men of the struggle.

'My mother and I are nobodies,' she said. 'My father died fighting for this freedom and the movement does not really care about widows and orphans. It doesn't.'

CHAPTER 3

Fezekile and South Africa's unfinished business

There is unfinished business in South Africa, on the political and economic front. Conversations about how our democracy has failed to guarantee economic freedom and equality are taking place, at least – all over social media, in academia, and on every single media platform there is. But the sexual violence that women and children endured in the fight against apartheid has not enjoyed the same attention.

What does this have to do with Fezekile and the famous rape trial? Everything. Unspoken apartheid-era abuses, on both sides, laid the ground for Fezekile's treatment. It is well worth pausing to consider these before returning to her story.

South Africa's Truth and Reconciliation Commission (TRC) did not have a category for gender violence against women. The unique violence – often sexual – that women faced was addressed under 'serious ill-treatment'; according to the Khulumani Support Group, an NGO comprising victims of apartheid-era gross human rights violations, this category also included solitary confinement. Khulumani has created a place of safety for the victims of apartheid-era rape to come forward and articulate their trauma. It holds regular workshops for victims of apartheid violence, from combatants to ordinary people. Some of these survivors are unemployed, traumatised and homeless. Some are ill. All have been forgotten; the wheels of the new South Africa have turned too fast for them to come aboard.

The women who came before the TRC were questioned about everything except rape. Gender researcher Nomarussia Bonase says that 'if a woman said it had happened to her, the interviewer often did not record it. When a woman did demand that their experience of rape be counted as an act of political violence, TRC statement takers told her that they would only include it if she reported the complaint to the police'.[4] This was an absurd idea, given that the police were also perpetrators of horrific sexual violence against women – both ordinary citizens and activists who were captured and arrested.

Nomarussia was born prematurely after her mother's gang rape by apartheid police. Her father was a miner, a member of the generation that provided cheap labour so that apartheid and colonialism could thrive. Miners, many of whom were sourced from the rural Eastern Cape, were housed at all-male hostels and visited their homes only when operations shut down – if they could afford to make the trip on their meagre salaries. These living quarters were detrimental to the black population's family structure, roots and sense of belonging. Families simply learnt to cope with being torn apart for long periods, a separation that birthed a normative culture or practice that still endures today – poor workers still leave their homes, spouses and children for months on end in search of work. How this impacts on the psychology of a society is a discussion for another day.

In defiance of laws forbidding women from visiting all-male compounds, Nomarussia's mother took a risk and visited her husband. He was on the night shift, and left his pregnant wife in his room one night. She was resting when apartheid police barged in in the middle of the night, kicked open the door and took turns raping her.

That was her punishment for being in her husband's room.

For her husband, it was an ominous message: he was not man enough to protect her. In the morning, he found her bleeding. With the help of some colleagues, he rushed her to Baragwanath Hospital, where she went into early labour. Nomarussia was born six weeks prematurely. She has spent her life as an activist in support of women like her mother – women whose bodies are a war zone, who are told, Don't talk about it.

In 1997, Professor Sheila Meintjes made a submission to the TRC and has repeatedly questioned the role of the TRC in its failure to address rape. In her submission, she states that '[o]f nearly 9 000 cases of violations (reported in the TRC commission to date) only about nine have claimed they have been raped. Yet in our research we came across many cases of violations which could be described as rape or where women knew of others who had been raped'.[5]

In a way, the rape of some women and children in exile debunks the heroic narrative of the struggle. It also debunks dominant patterns of self-glorification. The ruling party has, largely, been in denial about this, choosing instead a narrative that speaks only of the heroism and sacrifices of so many gallant comrades – a narrative that is true, but incomplete. The war against apartheid was fought on and across women's and children's bodies. Many paid the price.

Apart from feeble concessions, neither side wished to account for the sexual violence. Joe Modise, a senior MK commander who later became South Africa's defence minister, acknowledged the problem of rape and sexual harassment in ANC camps.[6] There was also a high incidence of transactional sex, where young women, who had left their homes to join the struggle, were promised scholarships, food and clothes in exchange for sexual favours. For some, the conditions in the camps were so bad that further military training or pursuing an education overseas was the only way they could survive; they would acquiesce to their commanders' persistent propositions. What made this particularly difficult to resolve was that these acts were perpetrated by senior commanders. While some ANC leaders have hinted at these abuses, when calls for an official enquiry were made, the ANC closed ranks. Some saw it as a ploy by opposition parties to score cheap political points. It seemed that it was far more important to ensure that the opposition did not prevail than to address this scourge and ensure justice for the many survivors.

It is not fair to describe all liberation camps as places where women were violated. Many women in the camps were treated as equals, and supported in exercising their agency. But the secrecy surrounding their experiences creates the impression that the liberators have much to hide.

At the Politics of the Armed Struggle conference at Wits University on 23–25 November 2016, gender was on the agenda. In a public dialogue, 'Fighting on Two Fronts: Experience and Practice of Gender Struggle within the Armed Struggle in Southern Africa', on 24 November, senior women who now hold positions in government denounced arguments that rape had been rampant in ANC camps. Judy Seidman, a cultural worker and visual artist, insisted that it had happened to shouts of, 'Where, where? We were there, where did these rapes happen?'

One contributor, Pumla Williams, went on to describe how women combatants were known as 'flowers of the revolution' precisely because their male counterparts protected them. She echoed Thenjiwe Mtintso when she said, 'I had a gun. I knew how to use it. No man would dare rape me.' This scenario is problematic in many ways. It diminishes the complexity of sexual violence and posits the gun as a preventative weapon. In saying that they had guns and would never be raped, these women fail to address the masculinist politics that give rise to all forms of gender-based violence. Had they not had guns, would they have fallen victim? I asked this question; it was never answered. The gun does not erase the vulnerability of a woman to abuse, harassment and rape.

The conference attendees seemed frustrated that their courage and bravery were muted by 'this narrative of rape'. This is understandable: many of them gave up their youth and took on dangerous missions in the fight for a democratic and free South Africa. They had agency and purpose. But to dismiss stories of rape, abuse and harassment is to be ahistorical, to delegitimise the women who say they did experience sexual violence.

My sense at the conference was that those in attendance were not happy with how women were portrayed – as victims of sexual violence; in defending their position, they inadvertently closed the space for any interrogation of the gendered nature of armed struggle. This is bizarre, especially in light of the well-documented link between rape and war on a global scale – a phenomenon that speaks to violent masculinities the world over.

As recently as 2016, former UN secretary general Ban Ki-moon released a report[7] that indicated that UN peacekeepers were committing widespread sexual abuse in various parts of the world. The report listed 99 different sexual assault allegations, in 2015 alone, against UN peace-keepers in 21 countries. The report also noted that the number of sexual attacks by UN peacekeepers had been increasing over time. In Bangui, Central African Republic, sexual predation was well documented, with women and girls raising the babies of the UN troops who had abused and exploited them. These are called peacekeeper babies. The UN troops have been formally accused of sexually abusing or exploiting civilians – mostly underage girls. The report documented how French troops, in particular, demanded oral sex from children, impregnated some women and children, and forced others to perform sexual acts in exchange for water and food. They understood the power that they held.

In TRC documents, there is the story of Rita Mazibuko, raped by colleagues in exile and threatened about speaking out about this at the TRC's Women's Hearings.[8] In her testimony to the TRC, she said she had often cooked for senior ANC leaders Mathews Phosa and Zola Skweyiya. It was recorded that she had worked for the ANC in Swaziland, but fell out of favour in 1988 when nine people were killed and she was accused of being a spy at the time when the organisation was being infiltrated. She alleged that, as punishment, she was raped and tortured repeatedly by her comrades.

The women of MK are proud of the title 'flowers of the revolution' – in articles and a documentary about this, they speak nostalgically about their role. Deconstructed, this term speaks of the fragility and tenderness of flowers – of the need for women to be protected and nurtured. Despite its good intentions, casting women soldiers as flowers reflects, directly, the ideological construction of gendered roles, with masculinity being strong and brave, and existing for the sole purpose of protecting femininity, which is fragile and pure, like a flower. In her paper 'Women, the military and militarisation: Some questions raised by the South African case',[9] Jacklyn Cock writes that '[t]his division – separating the protector from the protected, defender from defended – is crucial to both sexism and militarism'. She further states that:

> The role of women in militarisation has been largely obscured and mystified by two competing perspectives – those of sexism and feminism [...] As the weaker sex women must be 'protected and 'defended'. One variant of feminism similarly excludes women but on opposite grounds – that of their innate nurturing qualities, their creativity and pacifism. Another variant of feminism [...] excludes women on the grounds that men have a monopoly of power. The outcome of these perspectives is that war is understood as a totally male affair and the military as a patriarchal institution – the last

bastion of male power – from which women are excluded and by whom women are victimised.

This last part is pivotal. It is hard to believe that, in a world of enduring patriarchy and gendered militarisation, ANC camps would be unique military spaces where women were equal. The word 'flower' already makes women unequal. The question is, to what extent did this inequality, and the conceptualisation of women as flowers, create fertile ground for them to be 'picked', as it were?

The chairperson of the National Council of Provinces (NCOP) at the time of writing, and senior MK commander and operative, Thandi Modise, has spoken out about the two-pronged battle that women cadres had to fight. In an interview with Robyn Curnow,[10] she relates how they arrived at ANC headquarters in Tanzania as little girls, on a wave of revolutionary zeal. They received political education, which was emphasised over military training. But the reality of being a female soldier soon hit many of them hard.

Modise tells Curnow:

> There was this idea that we needed to be super-fit. Against the enemy, the South African state then, and against men who just wanted to take advantage of us. [...] But there had been a fight one night over girls ... because there had been a feeling among some men that because there are these five, six women there, 'Why should they be sex starved?' and there were others who said 'No, they are not here to be sex slaves, if they want to have affairs they will have affairs, if they don't want to, then you are there to protect them.'

Later, Modise and her female comrades were sent to the Angolan camp,

Nova Katenga. There were about twenty women to about five hundred men. Women stood no chance against harassment and the constant attention, often unwanted, from their male counterparts. It was worse when the attention came from senior commanders.

In Angola, an incident known as the Brushman affair further highlighted the vulnerability of the women and the sexual assault that many experienced. The doors in the women's barracks did not lock. At night, they were vulnerable and exposed. To Curnow, Modise said,[11] 'Day by day, you'd think, "Who do I talk to?" Because in the middle of the night there would be this hand fondling you.' The women realised that, every night, someone was – or some people were – coming into their private space and feeling and fondling them without their consent.

One day, the women had had enough. They planned a campaign to fight back. When the man attempted his assault, all twenty women chased after him, running and screaming. Most of the women were clad only in sleepwear or underwear, given Angola's oppressive heat. The physically strong culprit simply brushed them off and ran to safety.

His male comrades hid him. In their world view, it was incomprehensible to fight for the women. Their instinct was to close ranks and protect the perpetrator, because he was one of them. 'We wanted this man because he'd been fondling our bodies for months,' Modise says.

The next morning, the men in the camp were furious with the women, criticising them for not dressing properly before they gave chase.

Even the songs sung at the camps were rich with crude, sexist language. Modise tells Curnow of a traditional Xhosa song, sung before the slaughtering of a cow: 'How does a cow see when it is time to be slaughtered?' Some of the men in the camp would sing, 'How does a woman see when she is going to be fucked?' Suttner captures this succinctly when he writes that '[l]iberation struggles are suffused with masculine idioms and language. African men have described themselves as emasculated by apartheid; the struggle for liberation is described as one where men recover their manhood.'[12]

Modise concludes that camp leadership had not addressed the matter of what she called sexual harassment by the time she left the camp. But this went further than harassment. It was assault. Who knows how far it went in some instances?

These oral histories are crucial – to deny harassment and abuse is to deny the global scourge of misogyny. The desperation to sanitise the issue is just as problematic as reducing it to a narrative of abuse.

. . .

If, as it appears, the ANC in exile knew about the abuse of women and children by its comrades, what did the movement do about this knowledge, and was it enough to send a clear message that the ANC would not tolerate such behaviour?

Struggle icon Gertrude Shope has been out of the limelight for many years now. She trained as a teacher, but was pivotal in the campaign to boycott Bantu Education, an inferior education system that the apartheid government designed for black people.

Shope joined her husband, prominent ANC leader Mark Shope, in exile in 1966. Like many exiled families, they moved around the world doing ANC work in Botswana, Tanzania, Czechoslovakia, Zambia, Nigeria and Zimbabwe. Shope headed the ANC Women's Section and started a publication called *Voice of the Women*. Having settled in Lusaka, Zambia, she was sent by the ANC to its camps when allegations of sexual abuse emerged. She would have known Fezekile and Beauty.

When I phoned her daughter Lyndall Shope-Mafole – former Director General of Communications and now one of the founding members of the Congress of the People (COPE), a political party formed by a breakaway from the ANC in 2008 – I did not expect such a reception. She told me she was happy I was writing 'about this'. And that she could weep, because it was so long overdue.

Shope-Mafole grew up in different countries in Europe, as well as Zambia and Tanzania. She was one of the protected young girls, because her parents were the Shopes, both prominent ANC leaders. In exile, there was a class system. Some women were protected because of who their parents – their fathers – were. Many comrades have written, and still speak in awe, about MaShope's late husband. I sit down with mother and daughter to talk about sexual violence in ANC camps.

As a prominent woman leader in the ANC, it was MaShope's role to visit young female recruits and find out how they were faring and what challenges they faced. She did not dispute the version of any woman who says she was raped, but says that there was no deliberate attempt to silence women. She concedes that 'there were many who did not return from Quatro' – the infamous prison camp in Angola where many untold atrocities were committed by Imbokodo, the military leadership of MK. And Lyndall adds, 'There was a lot of discipline amongst the youth outside the camps, at the Solomon Mahlangu School and other youth networks. But maybe at the camps, there were things that happened. Yes, there were men who propositioned young women and it suited them to keep them at the camps so that they could have access to them. But generally, there were rules and strict discipline.'

Thenjiwe Mtintso is another ANC veteran, a close associate of Steve Biko who joined MK after being tortured by police in the 1970s. She rose to become MK commander in Botswana. In democratic South Africa, she worked for the newly established Commission for Gender Equality, which was no surprise: even in the masculine environment of the military camps, she was known to be an unwavering feminist who championed the cause of women and confronted patriarchy and sexism wherever they occurred. Mtintso was unflinching and held her own among prominent leaders of the movement. She left the Commission for Gender Equality when she was appointed deputy secretary general of the ANC.

I had read, in various reports, about how a young male comrade had threatened her with rape, telling her, 'You know, it's going to get to the point that I am going to rape you [...] and I know there is no way that you are going to stand in front of all these people and say I raped you.'[13]

If someone so senior was threatened with sexual violence, many others would have been too. Mtintso says some women combatants were deliberately set up in houses where the male comrades would 'visit' and 'sleep with' them. 'And that is rape,' she says. 'That for me is rape.'[14]

Some ANC leaders acknowledged these abuses, however. In fact, the ANC's own report to the TRC, which was submitted by then Deputy President Thabo Mbeki, acknowledged that men in camps had committed 'gender-specific offences' against their women comrades. According to Meintjes, the report says the perpetrators were punished, but their offences, nature of punishment and names are not known.

I meet Mtintso to clarify her position on, and recollection of, this chapter in the war against apartheid. I ask her whether there are any senior men in the movement who were guilty, which would explain the fear and silence.

'Yes there are, and some became very senior members of government.'

She is reluctant to name them – she does not want to open herself up to a lawsuit, especially since the perpetrators were not found guilty. She also confirms that some senior ANC/MK commanders may not be guilty of rape, but that they certainly – brazenly – used their position to control women and demand sexual favours in return for perks: 'Some of the young recruits were left in no doubt that, in order to get ahead, they would have to warm the beds of their seniors.'

One MK commissar – Andrew Masondo, imprisoned on Robben Island for twelve years and a senior leader of the ANC in exile – faced allegations of exploiting his position. Some rank-and-file members of MK accused him of abusing his authority, punishing those who did not follow his orders, and hoarding provisions meant for the combatants. But the most serious accusation against Masondo comes from former MK soldier Olefile Samuel Mngqibisa. He was part of a group that reported sexual harassment of young female recruits by iMbokodo, the Department of National Intelligence and Security of the ANC in exile. Mngqibisa says that Masondo was the director of the ANC's national school, the Solomon Mahlangu Freedom College (SOMAFCO), responsible for the education and welfare of teenage refugees from South Africa during the turbulent 1980s. He told an interviewer that 'Andrew Masondo impregnated a young SOMAFCO schoolgirl in 1989 and she had to abandon her studies. Masondo seriously abused human rights in the ANC. A majority of ANC girls who studied abroad used their bodies to get scholarships'.[15]

Incidentally, Mngqibisa wrote to me in mid-2016 when I was in the middle of my research for this book. I decided to meet with him, to see if he stood by his story. It was difficult to test the veracity of his claims: there were no records and Masondo had died, so the names of these young women were not known. Mngqibisa claims to have taken the statements from these young women, but that these were forcibly taken from him and that ANC leaders like Tim Maseko, Robert Manci and Stanley Mabizela thwarted any investigation into the matter.

When I met him, he stuck to his story. 'The sexual abuses were real,' he said. 'They can deny it all they want, but it did happen. They know and they know the leaders who did it, including Masondo.'

Mngqibisa spends a lot of time writing to newspapers, the ANC and human rights bodies, urging them to investigate these atrocities and demand accountability from perpetrators. 'I am persona non grata,' he says. 'The same thing that happened in exile is happening today; clos-ing ranks is far more important than doing the right thing.'

Women like Nkuli were abused not by senior leaders, but members of the rank and file. Nkuli left South Africa as a young woman to join MK. Now in her fifties, she is feisty and outspoken, with a strong sense of justice. She is among the many who gave up their youth to take up arms against a formidable enemy.

I found her by chance. I had mentioned on my radio show that I had an interest in apartheid-era sexual abuses, as perpetrated in liberation camps, apartheid police cells and township streets, saying that a cloud of secrecy surrounds the cross-frontier war fought on women's bodies. The next day, I received a visitor at reception: a young woman in her mid-twenties, who said her mother wanted to speak to me about her time as an MK soldier. She gave me a telephone number and address.

I called. We met, and spoke.

She remembers consuming alcohol together with two of her male comrades. It was jovial, and the camaraderie between them was com-forting. After all, they were in such faraway lands; to be accepted as one of the boys was a badge of honour. On the way back to the Dakawa camp in Tanzania, she says, 'We changed direction and I was taken to an isolated spot where my comrades raped me.'

She tells me she remembers being confused while it was happening, and asking herself how they had moved from being her brothers in arms to her rapists. 'It didn't make sense.'

She told them to stop. They giggled, and said she must stop being difficult. 'They were not aggressive or threatening, but the more I strug-gled the more they subdued me, telling me to not be cruel, not play around with them.'

'Nkuli, they were preventing you from leaving. Two men trying to pin you down – how is that not aggressive?'

I know the answer. What she means is that they did not beat her up or threaten her in any way. But sexual violence and rape need not be overtly violent.

Afterwards, one of the comrades said he was sorry.

'Did you accept that?"

'Not really. Thinking back now, I am fascinated that he thought he could say sorry and it would all just go away. He had no clue that they had just changed my life.'

'Did you say anything to any of them afterwards?'

'Not really. I had to live with them, side by side with them. Attend political school with them, do training, share meals. So, I just avoided them.'

'And I suppose you did not report them?'

'No, I could not do that. I had broken the rules by being out and drinking. We were not allowed to drink so if I related this "incident" I would have to confess to also being in the wrong.'

'But surely the scale of your transgression and theirs is incomparable?'

'I guess so, but I just did not want eyes on me.'

Exile and the camps themselves were small communities. Everyone knew everyone and there is no way that a hearing or 'trial' would happen in private. All her comrades would know that she had been raped; Nkuli did not want to live with that stigma.

I can also imagine that it was much harder to come out and expose the perpetrators knowing that the punishment would not suit the crime. It was too risky to involve the police: the ANC was already hampered by the presence of spies in its ranks, and was being intercepted on many levels. Bringing outsiders in to arrest and try its men would open so many of them to danger. So, the party functioned like a state, administering its own forms of justice and punishment that were often violent and cruel. Beatings, torture, isolation, denying food and water – this is how soldiers who broke the law were treated. For serious transgressions, such as accusations of being a spy, many were executed. Yet there was no such punishment for rape. Who would administer this punishment, anyway, when some senior leaders were also accused of gender-specific crimes?

So, Nkuli and many others just 'carried on with life'.

I also had a conversation with Prime Evil: Eugene de Kock, the apartheid-era police colonel who was the regime's most zealous assassin and head of the notorious Vlakplaas unit, named after the farm where activists were taken after their arrest. There, they were tortured, interrogated and killed. The likes of ANC lawyer Griffiths Mxenge and Siphiwo Mtimkulu were among the many freedom fighters who took their last breath at Vlakplaas – a name that still invokes fear and anger decades after being shut down.

De Kock and his men were not satisfied with just killing their victims. They would blow them up, or throw them into crocodile-infested rivers, all while having a braai and drinking to the stench of burning human flesh. It was grotesque.

At the dawn of democracy, De Kock was thrown under the bus by his colleagues and political masters who never accounted for their role in the torture and brutal killings of many black people. De Kock was one of the very few senior police officers who were jailed for apartheid crimes. Ironically, the country's new rulers embraced some of his colleagues. The system's most skilled engineer, it spat him out when it no longer had any use for him.

He denies that anyone was raped at Vlakplaas.

I could not imagine that such a dark place – where many died the most horrific deaths, where indescribable callousness was used to extract information – would not also have been a place of brazen sexual violence and rape. De Kock wants me to believe that women were only interrogated there. This was a war; rape has long been documented as a weapon of war, all over the world.

Major General Patrick Cammaert, former commander of UN peace-keeping forces in the eastern Congo, is quoted as saying, 'Warring groups use rape as a weapon because it destroys communities totally. You destroy communities. You punish the men, and you punish the women, doing it in front of the men. It has probably become more dangerous to be a woman than a soldier in armed conflict.'[16]

I could not imagine that a woman – seen as an enemy, on a farm in the middle of nowhere, surrounded by males who wanted to extract information from her and punish her for her politics – would just be left alone. But De Kock insists that no rapes took place at Vlakplaas.

I do not believe him, and I say so.

'No, none of that happened. Not under my watch. I draw the line at rape, especially of children.'

He tells me that, since his parole, he has been working with the National Prosecuting Authority (NPA) to bust child traffickers. Not only that, he is also assisting authorities and families of those killed by his men during apartheid. He has provided valuable information that has helped to trace unmarked graves and murder scenes.

But that is an entirely different story. Vlakplaas became a living hell. Nobody came out of there alive. There could be no greater power demonstrated by the apartheid state than to send a message to male freedom fighters by humiliating 'their' women. Yet De Kock swears that no rapes took place under his watch.

He is softly spoken, and I battle to hear him sometimes. He takes long pauses between sentences. And then: 'Maybe rapes took place in the vehicles, in open fields on the way to Vlakplaas, but not at Vlakplaas itself.'

'I see.'

He gives me names of his former colleagues, retired policemen and askaris who may shed light on the issue.

'Talk to them. They will tell you about the rapes, who committed them and ... you know.'

I see this as an admission that sexual violence was part of the apartheid state's machinery. Not that I believed anything to the contrary.

Even when apartheid structures were being dismantled, and the rainbow nation was being born, the sexual violence persisted. I meet a woman who wishes to remain unnamed. Her violation happened at the dawn of democracy. It is hard to imagine that, in 1993, Nelson Mandela had been out of prison for three years, and the foundation for the new South Africa was already being laid, yet the blood of so many was still spilling onto South African streets. The political violence on trains, in hostels and on the streets of South Africa claimed many lives in the early 1990s; 1993 was no different, and this woman knows that very well. The men who broke into her house were allegedly escorted by police. They shot and raped her.

A mere one year later, South Africans voted in the first ever democratic elections, which saw the iconic Nelson Mandela become the first president of South Africa. But, on the ground, the pain of so many remained unacknowledged, unspoken.

Busi Mthembu from Sebokeng, a township in the Vaal region, was another woman who paid dearly for her activism. She spent the 1980s in and out of hiding, and survived a lynching by fellow freedom fighters who thought she was a spy. Fortunately, another activist recognised her and managed to persuade the crowd that she was one of them.

Her luck ran out in 1990. The SADF broke into her shack and started hitting her in front of her children. She was taken to a police station about ten kilometres away. She can only estimate the distance as she was blindfolded and did not know where she was. She was asked to give information about ANC activities and names of prominent leaders in the movement. She refused, choosing death instead. She did die that day. A different kind of death.

'One of the policemen said to me, "You will never forget this day."' They took her to an open field and took turns raping her.

'There were about six of them, or seven. I don't know. It just did not end. It did not end.'

She was left for dead near a stadium. Passersby found her and took her to her shack, where her fellow comrades took turns taking care of her.

'There have been no reparations,' she says forlornly. 'No one has said, Busi, thank you for paying the price.'

'How would you like to be thanked? What should have happened?'

'Today, the women who did not go through what I went through, are the ministers with the bodyguards, you know.'

I am ready to leave it at that. But then she adds, 'They did not say sorry. They did not once say sorry. I want them to say sorry. And to say thank you.'

'The rapists from the army? So much time has passed, so many of them are no longer there.'

'I don't care about them. I am talking about our comrades. They did not say sorry for what we went through for our movement.'

'They may argue that everyone who was involved in the struggle paid the price.'

'The price? Everyone paid the price? The price of gang rape, strange men on top of you, ejaculating inside you, one after the other? I doubt it.'

She says she can still smell them on her body. 'You never forget it. Even textures.'

'Textures?'

'Yes, certain things you know, patterns, material, colours, sounds, they are everywhere and they remind you of the rapist. But mostly the smell. The smell is everywhere.'

(Fezekile told me that she had stopped watching television for years, because she did not want to see Zuma. When she saw him, she smelled him. But, she told me, as she reclaimed her power, she faced him, in newspapers, on television and on the radio. The sound and sight of him no longer terrified her.)

At about the same time that Fezekile was raped in exile, the jack-rolling phenomenon was playing out in townships. I am not suggesting that there were no township rapes prior to this, but the brazen, broad-daylight abduction of young women and teenage girls had never been seen before. The perpetrators were 'militant' youths, young men who ruled the streets of the township. Some called themselves comrades of the struggle, committing thuggery in the name of a just political battle.

The relationship between these men and their society signified very complex power relations. On the one hand, I believe they controlled the movement of young girls, often camping out at street corners, school gates and shops, ready to pounce on their victims. They objectified women, treating them as pieces of meat, unleashing their power and authority over their bodies. On the other hand, an understanding of the political climate of the time forces us to objectify the subject. Can the power and violence of these young men be divorced from their daily reality? Can it be discussed without delving into other problems?

The 1980s saw increased patrols by the army and police. Every day, there were police vehicles and army trucks in the streets, keeping a watch over unruly black folks. This created a highly charged environ-ment and, I believe, neutralised the traditional lines of authority and the leadership that may previously have been provided by churches, commu-nity elders, priests, teachers and parents. We witnessed adults whom we respected also being stopped and searched by police, sometimes beaten. Their authority, diminished so publicly. They ceased to have the aura and respect – and, dare I say, the power – that they once had. An atmosphere of war prevailed; belief systems and a way of life were disrupted.

Jackrolling was a political act reflecting militarised masculinities and patriarchal practices. I witnessed and heard about many jackrollings when I was a child. I know girls who were jackrolled. It wasn't difficult to know them – a peculiar feature of jackrolling is that it happened in broad daylight. A girl or young woman did not have to be isolated, or walk alone at night, to be at risk. The jackrollers wanted to be seen and known, and had no fear of being prosecuted. Why is that?

In 'Gang rape and the culture of violence in South Africa',[17] Lewis and Vogelman provide a possible answer:

> There are a number of aspects which make jackrolling different from ordinary rape. Firstly, it is primarily a youth phenomenon. Although rape is committed by males of all ages, jackrolling is committed by people who are still fairly young. Secondly, it is almost always committed in the open, and the rapists do not make attempts to conceal their identity. As a matter of fact, it seems that part of the exercise is to be as public as possible about the offence so as to earn respect.

These young people were establishing lines of authority and filling a vacuum that had emerged as a result of the bruising encounter with political power and its state apparatus: the army and police.

I meet Zanele, whom I found on social media. I sent a message asking for women who had been jackrolled, or who knew someone who had been, to email me. Within five minutes of my request, I had six emails. The trauma is unspoken.

A few days later, I meet Lerato. She does not seem persuaded by my argument that her rape was part of a political war. She says it was random, just a group of youths doing what they had always done, waiting for girls at a school gate. Township schools did not have multiple entrances and exits. There was one gate, which everyone used to come in and out. Besides, multiple gates would not have protected the teenage girls of Lofentse High.

Picture it, the brazenness. Boys in their late teens and early twenties, camping at the school gates, knowing that no one would stop them. Not the teachers, not the neighbours. They would get their way, as they always did. Lofentse was the only girls' school in Orlando East. It seemed to attract more jackrollers than any other school. That Lerato comes from Orlando East, where I grew up, is pure coincidence. Lerato was a pupil at Pace College, one of the best-performing schools in Soweto. Its principal was the legendary mathematician Dr Thamsanqa 'Wilkie' Kambule. He was also known for his vitiligo, which had turned him completely white. You could not miss him in a sea of black people.

On that particular day, Pace pupils had been given a study day to prepare for their mid-year exams. On a whim, Lerato decided to 'visit' her friends at Lofentse and walk back home with them after school. It was a bad move, she says.

'Why was it a bad move? You did not do anything wrong,' I say.

'I mean I should not have been there. *Ja*, that's what I mean.'

Is this not part of the misconceptions about rape? That women get raped because they make bad choices?

Lerato's life went on when the jackrollers were done with her, but she will never be the same again. Twenty-eight years have gone by. She is forty-five years old now, married with two children, aged nineteen and fifteen. 'My life is fine. I have not forgotten. But my life is fine.'

I know the answer to my next question, but I ask it anyway. 'Did you go to the police?'

'No.'

'Why not?'

She pauses for a while and answers, 'Jackrolling was in fashion. There were so many girls being jackrolled. They had no chance of solving my case.'

Poet and writer Makhosazana (Khosi) Xaba, a nurse who joined the anti-apartheid struggle after witnessing the cruelty of the apartheid state during student protests in Durban in the 1970s, relates an incident in which she was nearly raped as she got off the train while doing underground work. She was a trained soldier who would not have hesitated to use a gun, had she had one.

'I can handle an AK, make no mistake.'

'An AK-47? A real gun?'

She first laughs at my shudder – silly, really, because I know I am talking to a soldier, but guns have always terrified me. I don't get to finish my question because, in her loud, animated voice, she answers, 'Oh yes, a man who is about to rape me? I would shoot him.'

Khosi tells me about the dangerous circumstances under which female underground operatives worked. Unlike their male counterparts, they were often unarmed as they traversed the length and breadth of a hostile country whose government was hunting them down. On this occasion, Khosi was transporting money to other comrades on instructions from her commander Zweli Mkhize (ANC treasurer general, former premier of KwaZulu-Natal, and one of Fezekile's 'struggle uncles').

She says she had spoken to Mkhize about the need for a weapon, but he had not thought it was necessary as this was not an overtly military mission.

It seems to me that the leadership failed to grasp that, in addition to the dangers inherent in any underground work, women carried a double burden.

Khosi had strapped the money all over her body and was travelling by train one evening. A man alighted at the same station. She paid him no attention at first as he followed her out of the train station into an open field she had to cross to reach her destination. He pulled her to the ground and pinned her down, then yanked her panties down and opened his zip.

Maybe it was nerves, or pressure to get it done quickly, but he fumbled and battled to insert his penis. The irony of it: the impact on the rest of Khosi's life that this quick act would have had, had it happened. He became frustrated: his penis just wouldn't come to the party.

Khosi used this opportunity to break him down psychologically. She told him she had five children, all delivered through her vagina; that she was old, that her vagina was loose and tired.

'You are not going to enjoy yourself,' she told him. 'Think about it. Five children, all coming out of me. It is loose, overstretched, overused,' she kept saying.

The more she talked, the more frustrated he became. He tried to masturbate to get his offending weapon to become erect.

Khosi kept talking. Humiliated and embarrassed, he got off her and just ran away.

These are the women and girls whom the old country violated and the new one has neglected. In the old country, there was no point in reporting rape in police custody. Liberators and oppressors had something in common: their propensity for violence and demand for women's bodies. Two enemies, polarised by politics, yet in agreement that the female body was theirs to take.

Sexual violence was part of the DNA of the struggle. It is in society's DNA today.

Khosi gives me food for thought and challenges my casual extrapolation of the link between healing and talking. I am particularly passionate about the absence of women's voices in the struggle narrative. So many have written about their experiences. It is time for those voices to be heard. But Khosi asks, 'Heard by whom? By other women, who were victims themselves?'

'Heard from whichever platform, so that perpetrators know that victims are not hiding and will not give them the victory they want,' I suggest.

'It is difficult for women to claim space. It is a struggle, a negotiation. And in what format are women expected to talk?'

'Well, if they don't talk, then the violence goes unmentioned, unaccounted for.'

'But talking about it does not guarantee justice,' she says.

I know that too well from Fezekile's journey. 'True. But I cannot help believing that patriarchy and sexual violence demand our silence in order to thrive. That even when justice is denied, withheld, perpetrators must know that we know who they are and how they operate. At least some of these horrible experiences must be written about. If not to document personal pain and loss, perhaps to provide teachable moments for future generations?'

'Writing? Writing is tedious, even for me as a writer. And to whom must they talk?'

She has a valid point.

'Have you thought about the value of silence?' she continues.

'Huh?'

'Think about it. Keeping quiet in order to be secure – that was the modus operandi. Silence is complicated. It is negative at times, but if it keeps you alive, is it still negative? Even lying was a security measure, some form of protection. Do you know that as an activist, you lied to everyone – your friends, your family, your comrades? Little and big lies kept you alive. The less people knew about you – your weaknesses, your fears – the better. Do you know that it took me years to stop lying? I had to consciously and deliberately work at it. I had been so used to lying to stay alive. I had to unlearn that.'

So, lies kept you safe and created a layer that others could not pene-trate. Lying as security, protection – I had not thought of that in relation to sexual violence.

'Okay, but going back to the justice denied aspect: isn't the problem, here, that the silence and walking away comes from a belief that noth-ing will be done? And the silence and shame, while understandable, are the reasons why perpetrators entrench their power. The silence and shame are the reasons institutions do not transform and take sexual violence seriously.'

'I am not sure about that.'

A war, fought on women's bodies.

These women's stories share an umbilical link with Fezekile's own journey, laying the ground for her harsh treatment at the hands of patri-archal authority. Like them, Fezekile was supposed to live with it, put the movement before the self, lie supine before the authority of the male figures in her life. Instead, she disrupted the social order.

. . . .

CHAPTER 4

Forest Town

I learnt at Fezekile's funeral that she had a tendency to tell everyone her business. When she loved and trusted someone, she would tell him or her everything about her life. At the trial, my impressions were that this characteristic was used to ridicule her.

On Wednesday 2 November 2005, Fezekile sent several people whom she regarded as close to her the same SMS. In it, she told them that 'her child' – the son of her niece, Nokuzola – had been bitten by a snake in Swaziland and that she had to leave immediately to attend to him. Zuma was among the recipients.

Fezekile used to send me lots of SMSs. Lots. They were detailed, leaving me in no doubt about her state of mind. Whether happy or sad, she poured her heart out in words, which resulted in long messages. I was not the only recipient of these. As I talked to her friends and loved ones, we laughed loudly, comparing notes about the long messages sent to everyone and anyone she could think of at that time.

During the trial, this was presented as something special between her and Zuma, and thus indicative of some sort of flirtation. It is not unusual for her to have sent Zuma messages. She certainly could not have meant the affection in those messages as a sexual invitation.

Fezekile was so disturbed by the news of the snakebite that she was prepared to leave work that same afternoon and take public transport to Swaziland. In her version of that fateful day's events, Zuma discouraged her from going to Swaziland, inviting her, instead, to come to his house: there was little she could do for the child and, if the child was in good hands, the trip was not worth her effort.

His version is that she invited herself – to his Forest Town home, and into his bed. He testified to having talked her out of going, advising her not to travel alone, at night, and risk missing work for the rest of the week.

Zuma did tell the court that present on the evening of the incident were two of his children and Kadusha, whom he described as the child of a comrade who had visited him. In Judge van der Merwe's judgment,[18] in brief, we read that Zuma greeted Fezekile with 'Hello, big girl' on her arrival. Zuma finished his business with those present, and had dinner with Duduzane and Duduzile (his children), Kadusha and Fezekile. Duduzile then moved to take Kadusha home, and offered Fezekile a lift. According to the judgment, '[t]he complainant then said "I am not leaving, I am sleeping tonight". There was talk about a taxi because normally when the complainant visited the Zuma home she was picked up by a taxi'.

I have already mentioned that, even if this were the case, it would not have been unusual for Fezekile to assume that she was welcome there. Her life was spent mainly in other people's homes; she all too easily opened the door to anyone she cared for herself. Would a woman who wished to sleep over at a man's house with the intention of seducing or having sex with him say – loudly and confidently, in front of the man's daughter – that she was sleeping over?

They parted, according to Zuma's testimony, with him saying he had some work to do and her declaring that she was going to take a bath and then 'go to the room where she will be sleeping'. 'She', sleeping, alone, not 'we': a strange, cold 'flirtation'. She did not invite him to her room or indicate that she had anything further to discuss with him. Instead, he prompted the idea of a possible further interaction that evening when he said, 'Look, I am going to do some work and after that if there is still something to discuss then we can start discussing it.'

She replied that this would be fine.

When I first spoke to Fezekile, I had already read the entire court transcript – twice – and, with the help of a friend who is a judge, gone through questions that were purely legal and outside of the scope of this book, and those that were more psychological and social, reflecting the more complex layers of human interaction. Fezekile loved words, and rich, colourful descriptions. She was demonstrative and outspoken about her feelings. As a lover, she was passionate, decisive and fully engaged. This was a strange interaction for two people who allegedly fancied each other: from talking about snakebites, to declaring in front of Zuma's children that she'd be sleeping over, to discussing briefly her loneliness, boyfriends and HIV, to going to the guest room, to sex? Not a word of endearment, a compliment, a giggle here and there? They were alone. It was the perfect moment to kiss, to test the waters and send a clear signal for what was to come, what each was willing to do. Yet they moved from their boring conversation to him putting his penis in her vagina, with her consent?

Talkative, bubbly, sensual Fezekile? I don't believe it.

Incidentally, Adv Kemp ventured into this space when he asked Zuma, 'Mr Zuma can I just ask you at this stage, you had conversations in the past with the complainant. Would you describe her as a woman of a few words or quite talkative?'

In spite of myself, I laugh: I know there is only one answer to this question. It marks the only time, perhaps, that I have ever agreed with

Zuma about anything: 'She talks quite a lot and one would never feel lonely when she is there. She talks all the time.'

Judge van der Merwe continues:

> Once the accused had finished his work he went to the guest-room. He found the door slightly open and as the light was switched on he went inside. He found the complainant lying on her stomach on the bed with her thumb in her mouth, fast asleep on top of the bedding.

Fezeka was taken aback by my question. I had to ask it: 'Have you always slept with your thumb in your mouth?'

'Huh, *dade*, huh?' she laughed. 'How do you know that?'

'Mr Zuma said so, at the trial, that he had found you in the guest room of his home, sleeping, with your thumb in your mouth.'

'Mr Zuma said a lot of things. But *ja*, I do tend to do that. What does it mean?'

'I don't know. I really don't know. It's just that I do that, a lot.'

She got excited. 'Really? It must mean something. Why would two grown women do that?'

'Maybe we want to be babies again.'

Fezekile was wearing her famous kanga when Zuma found her asleep. She asserted that the rape happened in the guest room, where she was sleeping. Zuma insisted that what he regarded as consensual sex happened in his bedroom. It is widely reported that Zuma offered to 'tuck her in' and give her a massage with baby oil:[19]

> She said to him: 'I'm already asleep, I'll see you tomorrow.'
>
> Zuma replied that he could massage her while she was sleeping.
>
> She again said she was sleeping.
>
> Zuma then removed the blanket she was sleeping under.

'I was lying on my side. He started to massage my shoulders. He then held me on my shoulders and turned me around facing upwards. I then felt his knees on both sides of my legs.'

He once again started massaging her shoulders, 'and I said "no".'

'After I said this, he didn't stop massaging me. At that point I opened my eyes and saw that he was naked.'

She continued:[20]

'I thought "Oh no, uncle cannot be naked. He is on top of me and I am in his house." I thought "This can't be happening." And at that point I faced reality that I was just about to be raped.' She said he proceeded to rape her while holding her hands above her head.

Fezekile testified that Zuma ejaculated inside her, then went to take a shower.

In Zuma's testimony, as documented in Judge van der Merwe's judgment:

In his bedroom the accused was busy preparing the bed when the complainant entered. She was still wearing the kanga. She sat down on the bed. The accused took off his shoes and leaned against the pillows. The complainant again spoke about the child in Swaziland. She said she was getting cold and asked if she could get underneath the duvet. She did so. The accused then decided to put on his pyjamas and undressed in the room and put on his pyjamas. He also got into bed. The complainant then said that her body was tired and asked the accused to massage her. He fetched baby oil in the bathroom and started massaging her back while she was lying on her stomach. She loosened her kanga to allow him to rub her entire back and he noticed that she had no underwear on. He also rubbed her legs at the back and he noticed that she had no problem when he was rubbing her legs close to her private parts. She also asked him to massage her body in front. She turned around and the accused complied with the request. Once finished she thanked him, he washed his hands and came back to bed. In bed she covered him with her arm and as the accused noticed that something was now to happen he took off his pyjamas. When he got back into bed they started touching and kissing and eventually he asked her whether she had a condom because he had none. She did not have one. He said that he hesitated a bit which caused the complainant to say that he could not leave her in that situation and they continued to have sexual intercourse.

He said that he spoke to her during that process. She laughed and she said that she was fine and the discussion about the ejaculation took place.

According to the judgment, Fezekile then returned to the guest room, where she spent the night.

• • •

'When I saw the SMS, I knew something was wrong, but did not want to believe it. So, I tried to go back to sleep.'

Kimmy Msibi, whom Fezekile regarded as a sister, was the first person Fezekile told about the rape. I talk to her to understand what Fezekile must have been thinking that night.

'Why did you suspect something was wrong? I mean, it is strange to assume that an SMS automatically spells trouble?' I ask her.

'Well, she had sent me a message before that Malume is looking at her sexually. She was very uncomfortable. I knew she was in Zuma's house and was uncomfortable. Also, Fez was very strict about her sleep. She slept at ten. Every night, religiously, without fail. She was strict about sleeping at ten so an SMS from her in the early hours of the morning spelled trouble.'

Kimmy continued, 'We were sisters. We grew up together in exile. Both lost our fathers in the eighties. We went our separate ways, but found each other again in a free South Africa in the nineties.'

These relationships were precious. The war against apartheid caused untold pain, disintegrated families and friendships, and unravelled support structures. Relationships that had taken years to build were undone by the cruelty of the politics of the day. Fezekile and Kimmy's families were not immune to that; whereas some relationships survived exile and prison, they did not survive freedom. So, it was a poignant moment when the two sisters found each other again, and built a bond so solid that it would be a bulwark during the harsh times of the trial and its fallout.

The most annoying thing about living with Fez, Kimmy tells me, was her extraordinary neatness and cleanliness. 'We would eat and while I was relaxing, enjoying the aftermath of a wonderful meal, she'd get up immediately after the meal and clear the dishes. She took her last bite and literally dashed for the sink, with the dirty plates. I kept telling her to stop being such a clean queen. It was annoying,' she laughs.

Kimmy tells me that Fez was very open about her trauma from her childhood rapes. 'In true Fez style, she spoke openly about it. And every time she spoke she was sad. She allowed herself to be sad.'

But straight afterwards, Fezekile would become philosophical about those gloomy chapters in her life. She would say, 'I am going to put it into perspective. It happened. I must find the lesson in it. I am glad we spoke, I feel better and I look forward to a week of love.'

I smile. I witnessed a lot of these yes-I-can, I-am-a-conqueror moments. I am delighted that she found some relief and respite by talking to Kimmy. But I repeat an argument I made in my first book, *Endings and beginnings*: I cannot see what lesson that life, God, providence, or fate wishes to teach through rape. Why this lesson cannot be learnt without sexual violence and phallic victories, I will never know. I will never accept that our hearts, genitals and being need to be battered in the service of some celestial lesson. That there is a lesson that our brains and souls cannot grasp without this brutal violation.

Kimmy remembers an argument with Fez about the meaning of sexual violence. At that time, Fez was in therapy, seeing a psychologist who had said to her that she needed to make a choice about getting over her childhood abuse. Fezekile had a choice, the psychologist had said to her. She could carry the rapes in her heart and mind for the rest of her life, or 'Just think of them as a penis in a vagina. Nothing more, nothing less.'

Fezekile seriously entertained seeing the rapes through this reductionist prism. It felt, to me, that the psychologist was getting impatient, perhaps. But the fact that Fezekile kept going back to these chapters surely indicates the ineradicable impact of sexual violence on the victim or survivor's psyche? The inability to 'move on' speaks to the callousness of sexual violence; it is this cruelty that should be addressed, and not the victim's difficulty with rebuilding the shattered pieces of a life. Kimmy challenged Fezekile, saying that seeing it as just a penis inside a vagina minimises the pain and horror of sexual violence. I would add that doing so also absolves the perpetrators of responsibility and ignores the role of power in an act of sexual violence.

Kimmy and I discuss the silence about, and lack of accountability for, sexual violence that was a common feature of exile.

'There are things that happened, things that we did not talk about.

You did not tell your mother, you know, you were not brave enough to speak,' she confides.

'Why not?'

'It felt futile to report it. It was overwhelming. There were bigger things at stake and certain things had to be put aside.'

'Pain had to be delayed?'

'Yes. There was a war going on and maybe everyone felt, we will deal with it later, let's just get this bigger fight out of the way.'

'That seems so unfair.'

'It was very unfair. But, sad as it is, I have to think of it that way. Otherwise, it would be too traumatic for me to think that the adults around us were uncaring. I have to believe that they had planned to address it sometime, somehow. To think that they did not care ... well, that would be traumatic, devastating.'

But it must still be devastating to realise that there is a hierarchy of trauma and pain. Those who died in battle, who were captured and paid with their lives, have streets, halls, stadiums and other public places named after them. Yet those who paid with their bodies and souls go unmentioned.

Kimmy is deeply philosophical about the female body: 'It has always been made smaller than anything and everything. The female body has to wait – disappear, almost – while other, more important, things are being addressed.'

'Isn't it ironic, though ... that the war happens on the female body, with all sides of the war appropriating it. This demonstrates its importance. Yet, treating it like a mere piece of meat, violating it in this manner, means it is being made smaller, rendered worthless.'

Kimmy remembers Fezekile's confusion in the aftermath of the incident at Forest Town. Her doubting herself. Her wondering what she had done wrong. 'She wondered if she should have objected harder. I know

Fez. I believed her. When I spoke to her the morning after, I knew she was holding something back. She was just dull and spoke as if she had a lot on her mind. She did not immediately tell me, but I knew something had happened.'

This is interesting: at the trial, the defence argued that Fezekile's not telling Kimmy – not saying openly and clearly in the conversation with Kimmy – that Zuma had raped her meant that it had not happened and that she had thought about laying the charge only much later.

'Fez was like that. She liked to think things through. She liked to probe and verify and I know that, for a while, she was trying to figure out what on earth happened. She did not want to make any mistakes.'

It is not unusual for rape victims to be confused, especially when the perpetrator is someone trusted and respected. The law has to deal with facts; I wonder how much provision it makes for confusion and a sense of betrayal. Society has to decide whether this is the law's strength, or its weakness.

When they spoke again later that day, Fezekile was crying. 'She was manic. She was revolted.' That night, the two sisters sat on Kimmy's bed, with Fezekile talking continuously, asking herself over and over: 'How did it happen? What is it about me that makes me rapeable?'

Kimmy is emphatic. 'I know that Fez did not give consent. I know it. That night, I held her hand as she talked and talked, until I could not keep my eyes open any more. It was out of character for her. Yes, she talked a lot, but she let others talk, too. She had that distant look in her eyes, that enquiring expression on her face, like someone trying to make sense of something.'

'But I said no. I said, "No, Malume." I said it.'

Then, crying even louder: 'All day, all day, I could feel his sperm coming out of me.'

That night, the night after the incident, Fezekile could not stop speaking. There was no sleep in her. All her emotions were pouring out.

Kimmy confides, 'And when I got too tired, I dozed off but held her hand so that she knew I had not left her, and would not leave her.'

. . .

Fezekile laid a charge of rape against Jacob Zuma on 6 December 2005.

'I did not set out to change history. If that is what journalists and activists believe, then I guess they have a right, but I did not set out to do that. I just wanted to fight for myself, at last.'

I replied to Fezekile, 'In fighting for yourself, you did open a space. Maybe you were a catalyst for us to go where nobody wanted to go? Maybe a chance for us to have the conversation about male power, its entitlement and our complicity in aiding and abetting it?'

'My body was a soiled space, you know, from when I was a child. It was important for me that I say to him, you cannot come onto my body and just do what you want to do. And soil me like that.'

She reflected, 'I never saw myself as Zuma's accuser, Zuma's victim, or Zuma's anything. I do not want any attachment to that man. It is unavoidable, of course, because, when using my name, people have to explain who I am. But it was very interesting to me that I did not see myself as having all this power and yet, I was presented as someone who was so powerful that I could bring someone of his stature down. It had not occurred to me.'

'But taking action against such a powerful –' She interrupted me before I could complete my sentence.

'I did not think about that, his power, his position, that I was a nobody and here was someone powerful. I did not think about those trappings. This is what he did to me and I had to fight for myself. *Qha*! (That's all!)'

But, as the magnitude of her fighting for herself took shape, she was smart enough to realise that the event represented something significant for South Africa. It is common knowledge that the rape trial attracted a lot of attention and international media coverage. As much of this is already in the public domain, a great deal more happened that several key players are too afraid to discuss.

Immediately after laying the charge, Fezeka was surrounded by a lot of people, who turned out to be emissaries sent to persuade her to drop the charges. She could not distinguish between friend and foe; given her trusting and naïve outlook, she fell very hard. She came under enormous pressure. Aunties from exile were phoning and visiting her, asking her to drop the charge.

During the trial, she told the court about two specific aunties from exile, Mom Samkele and Mom Jane. Mom Jane was Kimmy's step-mom. Zuma testified that he had asked them to contact Fezekile and Beauty. The aunties arrived at 10 p.m. a few days after she had laid the charge, ostensibly to discuss her safety. They had travelled far. They expressed great concern for her well-being, but soon communicated the real reason for their anxiety.

'Mom Jane emphasised the fact that did I realise what this was going to do to the ANC, what it was going to do, it is going to rip people apart,' Fezekile recalled. 'She said to me, Could I imagine what this country would be like if Mbeki or Mbeki's people took over this country again? She said that I should just let it go.'

She says at that point she felt extremely pressured and had not prepared her mind for this.

'I was genuinely taken aback. I just did not think it would play out like that, with people I trusted just barging into my space and bombarding me. I mean, their great concern was the ANC and not me, their child.'

Even Kimmy came under pressure for supporting Fezekile. After being asked by one of the aunties why she was being so reckless, Kimmy answered, 'Auntie, you are like a mother to me. You all are our mothers. What if it was me? What if this had happened to me?'

The auntie replied, 'There is a bigger picture here. How dare you disrupt that? This was not a rape but an act of affection.'

For Fezekile, the most difficult aspect of the sordid affair was the vilification. 'Dear, it is the vilification that broke me,' she once said to me.

Journalists who had caught a whiff of the story were already circling. When Fezekile had been placed into the witness protection programme, Dumisani Lubisi of the *Sunday Times* called her to talk about the charge. She told him it was a sensitive issue that she did not wish to discuss. While she was on the phone with Lubisi, however, one Superintendent Khan was in the room. After a discussion with her boss, she instructed Fezekile to call Lubisi back and tell him that the rape had never happened and that there was no charge.

Fezekile did as she was told. Confined to witness protection, she had lost her freedom, authority and ability to make choices. She did not have legal representation at this stage; later, her legal team would advise her rather to enter the NPA's witness protection programme as the police were not mandated to provide the kind of protection she needed. In the ensuing confusion and fear, she had stuck with the police, believing that surely they were on her side.

Later that evening, Superintendent Khan came uninvited to Fezekile's room. She informed Fezekile that the *Sunday Times* was continuing with the story and that she needed to threaten them with legal action. Fezekile later told the court that Khan dictated a text message that she sent to Lubisi, recanting the rape incident. Khan then instructed Fezekile to phone a different newspaper, the *Sunday Tribune*, and speak to senior journalist (and, later, Zuma's biographer)

Jeremy Gordin. She was to tell Gordin that the *Sunday Times* would be printing a false story, and that she denied the rape. Gordin then asked if he could print Fezekile's name. Fezekile testified that Khan was constantly on the phone with her boss. Whoever was on the other side said that Fezekile must agree to her name being printed in the article.

The next day, Sunday 13 November, two major newspapers carried the story, with different accounts – one reporting a rape and a charge against Zuma, and the other denouncing the story and quoting Fezekile as having denied such an incident. The *Sunday Times* had refused to discount its original story, knowing all along that Fezekile was being pressured to deny that she had laid the charge. Knowing this, it is safe to deduce that a plan emerged from somewhere to get another newspaper onto the story, but that its angle would be an invalidation of the rape allegation and charge. In court, these two versions were used to depict Fezekile as unreliable and a liar.

When we spoke about this, Fezekile said, 'I had never felt so stupid in my entire life. They made it look like I was just a confused liar, making statements and withdrawing them. It wasn't like that.'

'They played you, didn't they? Fez, didn't you think it was just odd the way the police were so vested in what the media wrote or didn't write? I mean, did you not suspect that this was the beginning of the efforts to discredit you?'

'Ha, why are you so hard on me? How am I supposed to know how you media people and police work? And I was on witness protection. You follow instructions when you are in witness protection. Police have the overall say. And they told me that if I did not retract the story, it was going to be bad for the investigation, that it would compromise Zuma's rights and on that basis, he may walk. So, I did what I was told.'

I was genuinely flummoxed when Fezekile admitted that she did not know that, once she had laid a charge, the matter would automatically move into the public domain.

'The media had not crossed my mind at all.'

'You are joking.'

'Ha ha ha, no!'

Fezekile's world was very different from this one. She was not street-wise. She took everything at face value, trusted what she was told, and had no knowledge of a different world, a world where people did not mean what they said or do what they said they would do.

The pressure was insurmountable. The Monday after the articles were published, Fezekile and her mother received a call from Dr Zweli Mkhize, a senior ANC leader and trusted Zuma confidante who would later become the premier of KwaZulu-Natal under Zuma's presidency and, then, the ANC's treasurer general. The Kuzwayos knew Mkhize and were comfortable with him. It is in Fezekile's testimony that Mkhize called to talk about compensating the family for what had happened. Fezekile informed him that she was continuing with the legal process and that, if there is to be any compensation, then it must be discussed with her mother. She testified, 'He then said that the two processes could not happen at the same time.'

Fezekile's advocate, Charin de Beer, responded, 'What two processes is that?'

'He said that if they were arranging compensation then I could not carry on with the charge, I would have to drop the charges.'

Fezekile's account is that her mother told Mkhize that, according to her knowledge of Zulu culture, there was no compensation for rape: 'She did not know that such a thing existed.'

Zuma also phoned Fezekile during this time. It was highly inappropriate for the accused to call a plaintiff who was in witness protection.

No one aside from her lawyers and law enforcement should have had access to her. She still did not have legal representation, and was doing and saying everything without any legal guidance. Zuma wanted to meet with Fezekile in Durban, 'to talk about him and I'. She told him she would prefer to bring her mother to the meeting, to which Zuma responded positively – he also wanted to talk to Beauty.

In the end, Beauty did meet Zuma at his home in Johannesburg. She insisted that Zuma's senior wife, MaKhumalo, be in attendance. She knew MaKhumalo and wanted to speak to both her and Zuma; Zuma told her he would not be able to bring her to the meeting.

'That was just a cowardly act by him,' Fezekile said. 'He did not want his shame to be witnessed by MaKhumalo. He could not stand the idea of my mother telling his wife how disappointed she was in him.'

Beauty is petite and soft spoken. She was not intimidated by Zuma and his stature. She had known him in exile and had interacted with him on many occasions. On that day, she wanted to confront him about why he had done such a thing.

The meeting happened in his home – again, a reflection of power relations. He was the one facing charges, who had broken moral and cultural codes, yet they had to go to him, to his house, where he was lord and master. Beauty did face him and ask him why he had done it. The answer he gave her was not clear because, according to Beauty, 'he did not also know' (he did not know himself).

I imagine this was an opportune time for Zuma to give Beauty the same reasons that he would later give the court: that Fezekile 'had consented', that 'their relationship was of a sexual nature', that 'she had come to him', that 'in his culture it would have been wrong to leave her in that aroused state', that her 'seductive clothing', the kanga, was 'a sign that she wanted him'. Why could he not face Fezekile's mother and say these things? Why was he ashamed to own his truth?

Zuma apologised to Beauty, but he did not elaborate on what he was apologising for.

Beauty was not satisfied. She interrogated him: 'I know you, you do not take liquor and if you were somebody who drank, it would be something.'

What she meant was he had been sober – so, what could have possessed him to go after her daughter?

Beauty then told Zuma about the negative impact of this incident on Fezekile's health, that her CD4 count had gone down. She expressed the fact that she was particularly devastated because she had hoped Fezekile would pursue her studies in England, but this incident had set her back. Zuma offered to make arrangements for Fezekile to go to England. In court, Beauty said she declined the offer – she was not greedy and, besides, Fezekile had all but given up hope of going to school. In court, this matter was presented as something that Beauty had initiated – that she had demanded this as part of the compensation. According to the defence, Fezekile had also previously asked Zuma for money to erect a fence around their home, something she vehemently denies. Beauty told the court that, at their meeting, Zuma had offered to give them money for the fence as well. This was also presented as something that the Kuzwayos had requested of him.

Beauty did eventually agree to accept funds for Fezekile's education, but only if the money was deposited directly into the institution's bank account. She did not want to be insulted and accused of greed: 'To me, this man's money was not equal to the torture or the abuse on me or my child,' she said.

At the end of meeting, Beauty seemed to offer Zuma some redemption. As she told the court, 'When I found him at home on that day, he was very sad, disappointed, if I could use the English word M'Lord which will be appropriate, I would say he was sombre.'

Beauty encouraged Zuma to be strong, a strange change of heart given that she had come there to confront him. But she says she had done so because 'when somebody has said: I am sorry, I felt a bit of relief after he had apologised and apart from that, and as I looked at him, seeing the way he appeared at that very time, up till now I thought he was really sorry.'

'Up till now': until the trial, Beauty had believed that Zuma was genuinely sorry. But in the events leading up to the trial, how she and her daughter were hounded out, insulted and mispresented, it dawned on her that Zuma was not sorry.

. . .

Their phones did not stop ringing. With every ring, the pressure worsened.

'I was a nervous wreck,' Fezekile recalled.

She was invited to a meeting with an attorney whose name she battled to remember even in court.

'Who was this attorney?' Adv de Beer asked.

'He said he was Yusof?' Fezekile answered.

The lawyer, according to Fezekile, had been sent by Malume Zweli (Zweli Mkhize). Fezekile was relieved that at last she was speaking to a professional who understood the law and would ensure that she was protected. She, Kimmy and her mother met with him. His name was Yusuf Dockrat.

'After taking the story he then proceeded to talk about the case and the pros and cons of going on with the case.'

'What was he trying to do?'

'Initially he seemed to be objective and just talking and helpful and then towards the end of the conversation he clearly said that he was advising that I should drop the charges and when we finished talking it was clear that I said to him that I was not dropping the charges, he then just said that Malume Zweli would be surprised at the outcome of the meeting.'

'But Fez,' I interjected, 'you knew Mkhize and Zuma were close, you said that in court, you and your mom knew him but were not close to him. Were you not curious about why he would send this lawyer to you and your mom? Didn't you ask what the role of this lawyer was, who was paying for his services?'

'Malume Zweli sounded genuine, so it was easy to trust him. He also, at some point, came to see Ma, to see if she was coping, helped her with travel arrangements, money for food ...'

Even then, Fezekile could not bring herself to accuse Mkhize of foul play. But she remembered clearly that Mkhize had sent Dockrat and that the latter was intent on getting her to drop the charge. This claim would later be confirmed by the regional police commissioner and investigating officer in the case.

Late one night, alone at the 'safe house' she wrote in her diary:

> We were also discussing the lawyer Yusuf with mama, and how he did a very good job of making us feel like he was impartial and on our side, that he was not actually saying that I had to drop the charges. They definitely picked the right man for the job. He would have got me if I didn't know what I stood for. They are trouble, anyway, especially him coz he knows it is a state case, I don't need a lawyer.

Fezekile was played. She implies that she knew all along what was happening, but she didn't. She accepted Dockrat's bona fides without question and was relieved to have him. True, she did stand her ground and refuse to let him persuade her, but at that time she did not know that she did not need him. That became apparent when a prosecutor was assigned to her case.

These were big players: mother figures, a lawyer, police management, two men whom she regarded as uncles and who also happened to hold very powerful positions, all phoning her, one after the other, disguising their cajoling and subtle bullying as concern. When Adv de Beer questioned her in court about these events, it emerged that, when they happened, Fezekile had no credible legal advice – just police telling her to do this and that, a lawyer whom she had not appointed, and journalists pressuring her. The power relations were being mobilised; Fezekile's equilibrium was the immediate casualty.

'Every day, I felt fear. Every single day, I felt fear.'

'I am looking at your diary and it seems to me you just vacillated between hope and despair, strength and weakness.'

'Emotionally, it was taking its toll. Kimmy was on medication, I was on medication. I could not sleep. I did start to wonder if I did the right thing, dragging everyone into this. My mother was worried that someone would get hurt physically. It was too much.'

Her anxiety was exacerbated by a sense of foreboding at the thought of parting with Ma, which she was told she would have to do when she started testifying – Beauty was also going to testify. She wrote in her diary, a month before the trial: 'This, I tell you, will be the death of me. They know how much being with my mother means to me right now. I just can't cope without her. I worry about her worrying about me and that makes her ill.'

They said she could bring a friend to stay with her, but it would not be the same. She feared that whomever she brought to take Ma's place would be frustrated staying in the house all day, day in and day out.

Yet some days she would feel strong, optimistic and determined. On the eve of the trial, she wrote:

> *Izolo* [last night] I slept like a baby and had beautiful dreams in which I was with people that I love. This left me with a warm feeling inside. I generally felt as though I had been ready to go on the stand the first time and now am less ready but I feel all right. It is good to be all right. I am going to be just fine.

She could never have imagined what lay ahead.

. . . .

CHAPTER 5

On trial

Ten years after the trial, do we remember the questions that were posed to 'Khwezi'? In what ways did the questions themselves reflect society's institutions of power? In a rape trial, the victim is as much on trial as the perpetrator. Fezekile was on trial: every question put to her ensured that. The questions went even further – they entrenched misconceptions about consent and how it should and should not be communicated.

Jacob Zuma's rape trial began on 6 March 2006 in the Johannesburg High Court. His supporters, clad in ANC colours, some toting hateful, incendiary placards, massed outside. As part of the psychological warfare to which Fezekile was exposed during the trial, this was the gauntlet that Fezekile had to run to enter and leave the court. Her advocate had specifically asked that she be let in through the basement where she would escape the crowds baying for her blood outside court. This drill had been agreed to, and rehearsed over and over. Yet she was paraded right in front of the crowds, and taken through the entrance nearest to the mob.

By the time she took the stand, she was demoralised and frightened. She told me she had expected a bullet to land on her body from any direction; she had no doubt there were plans to harm her.

While the eyes of the world were focused on the trial itself, a power

Supporters of Jacob Zuma outside the Johannesburg High Court

Jacob Zuma's supporters in a show of loyalty during the trial

struggle between the NPA and the police played out behind the scenes. By this time, Fezekile was rattled and unsure of herself, but she decided to trust the police. She was assigned a bodyguard, Leila, who was with her all the time – except when Fezekile needed her the most – and attended Fezekile's sessions with her legal team and her psychologist. In her diary, Fezekile wrote that the police team assigned to her constantly fed her false information about her advocate and her abilities, asking her what they had discussed that day and why she was trusting a white woman to defend her.

Adv Charin de Beer was vehemently opposed to Fezekile's being kept in the police's witness protection. She felt strongly that the NPA's programme was better suited – unlike the police's arrangement, very few people would have access to her there. But a rapport had developed between Fezeka and the police guarding her. She had given them her trust. She had no confidence in the NPA's witness protection programme because the police had told her that the government was about to cut the NPA's funding; in no time, the witness protection programme would be discontinued. That was a brazen lie, but Fezekile bought it. She would later record her bitter regret for not trusting her own legal team and not following Adv de Beer's advice.

Leila may always have been present when Fezekile met with her legal team, but sometimes – at night, at the safe house, when Fezekile was alone and frightened – she would disappear. Still, it did not take long for Fezekile to become attached to Leila and feel very safe around her. This was vintage Fezekile, attaching very easily to people who showed her any sign of compassion and affection.

The police advised Fezekile to allow Leila to record all her preparatory consultations with her legal team and all her sessions with her psychologist as, according to Fezekile, 'these would help [her] to strengthen [her] case and ensure that [her] original words were recorded accurately, in case the court was misled or [she was] asked things that [she] cannot remember'. They specifically told her not to inform her legal representative about the recording, and assured her that the recordings would be made available to her at a later stage. Yet Fezekile did not think there was anything odd about police instructing her not to share information with her lawyer. Adv de Beer was not entirely happy with Leila's constant presence, but Fezekile insisted that she felt much safer with Leila around.

Leila had a backpack with her and would take it everywhere, even when she left the room for a moment. Fezekile says Leila sometimes popped out to change the recording device's batteries. Adv de Beer would continue talking to her client, knowing neither that they were being recorded nor on whose instruction.

I shook my head in exasperation. I cannot help judging Fezekile and, to be honest, being momentarily annoyed with her, so many years later.

'Come on Fezeka, man. Really? Did it not strike you as odd that the police were insisting that you do something behind your advocate's back and withhold such crucial information? Surely, the one person who was fighting your case in court needed to know?'

Even before the trial started, so much of what she had discussed with her lawyers had been recorded. She wrote in her diary:

> I have asked Leila twice for the tapes that were made for me to review sessions with Charin [de Beer]. She eventually asked me to ask the Commissioner and when I did he said first that he did not have them and had been under the impression that Leila had given them to me then he remembered that since they were in his safe, his secretary would not have given them to Leila without his instructions. He said he would give the instruction and I would get them. Well, more than two weeks later after being told that the director Zwelibanzi Nyanda would now be in charge of our safety, I asked him [the director] and he said that he had been in charge of making the tapes audible and on asking the commissioner, had been told that the tapes were my personal things and I had said that I didn't want them any more and so he [the director] had had them destroyed … ha ha ha … I guess that ends the story with the tapes.

My sense from reading this is that, when Fezekile wrote it, she did not realise the enormity of the missing tapes for the trial. The last sentence of her diary entry clearly demonstrates that she did not fully grasp that confidential consultations with her lawyer had been recorded and had now gone missing. This would have been an opportune time to inform her advocate, but she did not. By the time she realised what was going on, it was too late – she had been compromised.

91

She apologised to Charin for not informing her about the recording, but, again, it was too late.

During the trial, Fezekile was kept in different safe houses, and was moved regularly. One evening, she went to bed, leaving police personnel at their stations at the entrances and various points of the premises. In the middle of the night, she was disturbed by a sound. When she related the story, she had forgotten where the sound had come from, but the disturbance was such that she awoke startled. She got out of bed to check what it was, confident that police officers were present. She left the bedroom and the found that the lights that had been switched off were back on.

Every door in the house was wide open. There was not a police officer in sight.

She screamed, then called Adv de Beer in a massive panic. De Beer made a few calls; later, the police returned, giving no explanation for where they had been and why they had left their stations, leaving her alone in the early hours of the morning, a few hours before she was to take the stand and face what she described as 'the biggest fight of [her] life'.

The fight was a war. It seems that every weapon imaginable was used.

It was not the first time that Fezekile had been left exposed. A diary entry from before the trial says:

> Oh, before I forget, it's shortly before 11 a.m. and Leila still has not pitched, she didn't sleep here and she didn't inform us of the fact. Can't be certain, but I think it's the second time since we got to this woodlands area that she has not slept in the house. Anyway, the forces of nature are with me so I feel safe, maybe even safer and happier when she is not here than when she is.

Added to that, on the morning of the start of the trial there was no water in the safe house. Fezekile was frustrated. She remembered that she had told one of the officers guarding the house that a warm bath always relaxed her and helped her feel calm and confident; in fact, she wrote in her diary that:

> First thing I will do tomorrow morning is to run a bath and send a plea to the universe, to carry me, to watch over my mom and all the people who have sacrificed so much, their safety, their dignity, their everything. Water is healing. I will take a warm bath and stay there for at least an hour and wash away all fear and anxiety.

Years later, she believed it was a deliberate act. I am inclined to agree – that this was another weapon in the psychological warfare arsenal.

I have mentioned before that friends and family, with whom Fezekile had stayed long before the trial, say she hated wearing clothes when indoors. She would wear a kanga or, when completely comfortable, she'd be in the nude. Even at her funeral, Auntie Bunie said that one thing they both enjoyed doing was to walk around the house, going about their business, totally nude. Fezekile also liked to sit on people's laps, or give them an impromptu massage or a pat on the shoulder. She was generally affectionate. In witness protection, pictures of her were taken without her knowledge, recording these moments of her being particularly affectionate and playful towards the male officers. She behaved in exactly the same way with the female officers, yet somehow those images did not emerge. She loved to dance as well, and saw it as a sort of meditation. Pictures of her dancing, taken without her knowledge, played into the defence's strategy of depicting her as a loose, flirtatious woman who used her sexuality and nudity to lure men.

Fezeka alleged that, on one occasion in the safe house, one Commissioner Mpego asked her to come and sit on his lap. He would 'jokingly' refer to her as his girlfriend. Fezekile initially thought it was harmless fun, but apparently the giggles and playfulness between her and members of the team were being recorded. As time went by, Fezekile noticed that, when she was in Adv de Beer's presence, Mpego did not play this 'girlfriend game'. What was odd, she says, was that, 'Just the previous day in the briefing he had played it big time, even suggesting that I sit on his lap and later in front of Sup. Linda, talking about *lobola*.'

This made her suspicious. She made a mental note to create some distance between herself and Mpego. She related everything to her mother when they spoke; Beauty reprimanded her for letting her guard down again.

'I had not thought of that, you know, that I could not be myself. I was being asked to consciously not be myself.'

I sympathise with Fezekile. We live in a world where women are constantly policed and told not to act in a particular way – not to wear certain clothes, lest they tempt their poor potential abusers. These potential abusers have no agency or self-mastery, and cannot distinguish between right and wrong. They have assumed authority over women's signals and what those signals mean – and they always, conveniently, seem to mean an invitation.

At the time for which the trial was scheduled, Judge Bernard Ngoepe was judge president of the Transvaal Provincial Division of the High Court and a respected member of the bench. Zuma's defence had brought an application for Ngoepe to recuse himself from the trial, because he had authorised search warrants related to corruption charges against Zuma, which were still before the courts at the time of the rape trial. Judge Ngoepe recused himself because he wished to protect the judiciary's credibility.

Judge Ngoepe's two deputies were the obvious next choices. Judge

Jerry Shongwe had to recuse himself as Zuma had had a child with his sister. Next in line was Judge Phineas Mojapelo. The prosecution tells me he was dressed in his robes and ready for the trial when, inexplicably, he was replaced by Judge Willem van der Merwe.

Judge van der Merwe, the judge who had sentenced apartheid assassin Eugene de Kock to a lengthy prison sentence, stepped in. This is in no way a criticism of Judge van der Merwe's probity. It is true that his rape trial judgment was criticised by many; his peers have described his decision to allow cross-examination of Fezekile's sexual history as unprecedented. He was also criticised for dismissing evidence that Zuma had pointed out the guest room, and not his bedroom, as the scene of the crime. Less than a year after Zuma became the president of the Republic of South Africa, Judge van der Merwe was promoted, becoming deputy judge president of the Transvaal Provincial Division of the High Court. He may well have deserved the appointment, but it is not irrelevant that he acquitted Zuma. Sadly, even those whom Zuma appoints deservingly cannot escape scrutiny; he is, after all, the most scandal-prone president South Africa has ever had.

Fezekile was not required to be present in court throughout the trial, and I was surprised by how much of the trial she had missed. Her testimony and cross-examination happened away from the cameras. She tried not to follow every aspect of the trial obsessively; often, when I referred to someone's testimony, she was surprised, seemingly hearing it for the first time.

'It would not have helped to follow everything that was said. I came in and gave my side. I listened to some of the lies and distortions only if my advocate said they were relevant. Otherwise, I wasn't there every day and tried to avoid all that psychological damage.'

News about the trial did reach her, however. Some of the police officers guarding her would talk about the trial and sometimes leave newspapers lying around, where she could easily see them. This, too, was an attempt to unsettle her, I believe.

Although she was anxious and frustrated about her isolation before and during the trial, her diary entry on the eve of the trial shows her to be focused and determined:

> I think that what I will do is take it one step at a time. First get through the court case, whatever that brings (of course I hope we win, that the truth prevails and justice is done). Then I can deal with the other stuff more clearly, removing the man who raped me from my father and my father from the man who raped me ... I am hurt that he did that, disturbed by what he has done to our relationship, to the memory of our fathers. I'm disgusted by the thought of him on top of me and sweating and ejaculating inside me. I am confused by him looking at me as anything other than a daughter.

And, in an emphatic moment of self-actualisation, she declares: 'As long as I am clear in my head, which I am, that none of it is my fault. I did NOTHING TO BRING IT ON!!! I am not responsible for his behaviour.'

With these words, in a society so rife with sexual violence, Fezekile speaks from the grave, addressing the many survivors of rape and sexual violence, removing, on their behalf, the burden that masculinity has placed on all victims of rape.

· · ·

Just as this book is neither an exhaustive nor an authoritative account of Fezekile's life, it does not intend to give a comprehensive account of the trial itself. It would be beyond the scope of this book to give such an account. I contend, however, that some key themes of the trial – the concept of consent; freezing as a response to trauma; a rape victim's sexual history; the honeytrap conspiracy; and Fezekile's mother's testimony – deserve closer scrutiny, which I set out to do in the rest of this chapter.

On the fourth day of the trial, Adv Kemp J Kemp produced a copy of Fezekile's diary, much to her shock. He used Fezekile's accounts, there, of her childhood rapes in exile to question her understanding of the concept of consent. Undermining Fezekile's assertions that the childhood rapes had not been consensual was a key tactic in convincing the court that she had engaged consensual sex with Zuma.

Kemp's line of questioning is precisely what problematises consent and its opposite. It is a reflection of a lack of imagination and depth when conceptualising and understanding sexual violence and, by extension, power relations between perpetrator and victim. When a rape is not overtly violent and the victim does not scream, society battles to understand that such an incident constitutes rape. Add to the mix the fact that the victim willingly went to the premises of the perpetrator, and society, in general, sees this as consent.

It is not that simple.

In her diary, Fezekile wrote of her rape at age twelve:

> Thinking back now it was not very rough, not that that counts for anything, but just having heard of and seen footage of rape in comparison this one was not rough. He was thrusting and I had started to try to wriggle him off me. He asked me what the matter was and I said he should stop, that it was painful. He stopped. I got out of bed.

Fez was correct to say that the fact that it was not very rough does not count for anything. Many grown-ups who sexually abuse children do not necessarily rough them up or beat them. In her book *Rape: A South African nightmare*,[21] Pumla Dineo Gqola debunks the dangerous myth that perpetrators are monsters who are abusive all the time: 'This is an expectation that many people have, and consequently one of the most enduring rape myths. It rears its head often when a survivor's narrative is being questioned. Rapists and other abusers are normal people. They can be very loving and gentle to those close to them [...]'. Godfrey 'was not rough.' He stopped when Fezekile asked him to. But that, being an adult, he believed he was entitled to her twelve-year-old body is jarring.

The language in the account of five-year-old Fezekile's rape, as used in court by Zuma's advocate, also gets interesting: 'In this instance you relate an incident where a man in his early thirties [...] raped you as you say in here when you went over to their house [...].' What is the purpose of 'as you say in here', if not to make Fezekile the little girl's version contestable? To say, this is what she says but is not necessarily what happened? This granular detail – 'as you say in here' – is an invitation to the court to start entertaining the idea that an incident dating back some twenty-six years is what Fezekile says happened, rather than what actually happened. Given that the court has no way of concluding this either way, it is interesting that an incident which would have no chance of jeopardising or enhancing Zuma's case is being manipulated to cast doubt on a five-year-old's version.

The next part of the sentence is even more telling. Kemp says that Fezekile's attacker 'took off your clothes, took you into his bedroom and had sex with you'. Not 'raped you', but 'had sex with you'. That the court did not gasp at the thought of a man in his thirties 'having sex with' a five-year-old child is staggering. Earlier, when Adv Kemp used the word 'rape', it was prefaced by 'as you say in here'. But, when Adv Kemp uses the words 'had sex with you', they are not attributed to

Fezekile, but are counsel's own words. Already, the stage is set for the contradictory versions of rape vs consensual sex. I emphasise again that the 'you' in this case is a five-year-old child and the man in question is in his thirties.

The defence did not argue that Fezekile's rape by Godfrey did not happen – rather, it argued that it happened with Fezekile's consent.

Again, the question that should be asked of us is, why can a little girl not get into bed with a close adult male and trust that she will be safe? Why is it a given that 'something will happen' or she is 'willing for something to happen'? I anticipate that many will see this incident as bizarre. But is it? At some point, little girls grow up and stop bathing in front of their fathers, brothers and uncles. It is a transition that many of us make. But, at the time when we are in our children's bodies and not aware of our own sexuality, Fezekile's scenario with Godfrey is common, and not inconceivable at all. What should cause shock and be inconceivable is an adult male's believing he is entitled to a child's body simply because the child is there, in his bed.

For all the months when young Fezeka was getting into bed with Godfrey, in front of her mother, what was he thinking? That she was trying to seduce him, in front of her mom? The incident with Godfrey is particularly instructive in that it reflects the many complex layers of sexual violence and the brazen exercise of power relations. Godfrey asked her what the matter was – unusual, I suppose, for a rapist to enquire after a victim's well-being. This proves Gqola's point about rapists sometimes being caring human beings. But is it less of a rape because the perpetrator asked what was wrong? That he stopped when Fezekile told him it was painful? Is it?

She was a child, and he an adult. That is the beginning and the end of it. It is not her presence in his bed, often in front of her mother, that should cause alarm, but rather his belief that her presence in his bed meant that he could, and she wanted him to, penetrate her.

Adv Kemp's next question is exactly what is tragic and wrong about society's grasp of sexual violence. It is the reason why so many children live with scars that will never heal – the reason why so many of their adult violators walk around unrepentant and smug, assured of their comfortable place in a society that wipes away their shame.

'Now you have just been woken from sleep by him getting your clothes and your underwear off and after his having intercourse with you at the age of 13 [...].' Here is that language again, language that automatically denies Fezekile her legitimacy and believability. It should not be possible for grown men 'to have intercourse' with thirteen-year-old children. When they do, there is a name for it: rape. In the absence of legal definitions, does it not offend our senses that an adult man thinks he can 'have intercourse with' a twelve-year-old, going on thirteen? Adv Kemp does not cringe when saying these words – there is no sense from his disposition that this may in any way reflect badly on males who 'have intercourse' with children. He is, from the very beginning, reluctant to use the word 'rape'. He seems assured that he can badger Fezekile and question her about her childhood conduct. Why is he so confident that this will reflect badly on Fezekile, and not the adults around her? Could the court be a deeply patriarchal space too?

The line of questioning continues to reflect dangerous beliefs about rape and how victims should behave.

'You did not freeze?'

'No, I did not.'

There isn't a standard behaviour, or set of behaviours, that must be displayed for rape to have occurred.

About the incident where Fezekile says she was virtually kidnapped, bundled into a car and taken to Mashaya's house, Adv Kemp says that Mashaya 'took you to his house and it seems on the probabilities had sex with you'. She was thirteen years old.

Adv Kemp and Fezekile get into an exchange as he challenges her assertion that what happened was without consent. Adv Kemp says Mashaya will testify that what happened in his house was consensual. Fez rightly responds, 'I was 13 years old and any sex with any kind of consent at that point would not be sex at that age [...] I [would] not necessarily [...] have known what I was doing or understood the situation because I was young.'

Adv Kemp tells her not to worry about that, but to answer factually whether there was consent or not: 'Ms Kuzwayo, I take note of that, I want an answer from you on the factual issue, do not worry about what the legal position is. Did you consent to this or not?'

Fezekile says she was crying and kicking and screaming, and that she did not want to be in that house.

This is where the chasm between law and justice becomes most obvious. Adv Kemp knows the law; he does not need a lecture on it. But, by elevating a factual argument about whether Fezekile consented or not, and basically arguing that the legal definition was not relevant in this case, I believe he put Fezekile at a disadvantage. She was being asked to ignore what the law says about consent, to ignore that the law says a child cannot give consent, and focus on whether or not she had given consent. That she did not have the maturity, the emotional capital, to give consent should be relevant, but it wasn't. The legal process demonstrates its limitations by failing to appreciate the politics of power and how they are skewed in favour of the adult male.

I also find it perplexing that Mashaya was prepared to come to a court of law and publicly testify that 'he had had sex with' a child. Were he and the lawyers oblivious to the enormity of his admission? It should have caused ripples of shock, condemnation and pain – yet so confident was he that his behaviour was not abhorrent that he was willing to come forward and tell the world that he was a grown-up who 'has sex with' children. He could do this because he knew society's complicity in the violation of children. He knew he could confidently affirm that he 'had sex with' a child because his male privilege was guaranteed and the power relations – inside and outside that court – would protect him. He would not face scorn and derision because normative practices legitimised his conduct.

Adv Kemp then asks Fezekile: '[Was] your clothing removed by force?'

Fezekile does not remember.

'Would you know afterwards whether any of your clothing was torn?'

'I do not think anything was torn, no, no.'

I cannot say there was no basis for this question because I do not know what Adv Kemp knew. However, in as far as the question reflects a misconception about rape, it misses the point dangerously. So many victims walk away because they do not reflect the perfect picture of what a rape scene, and victim, should look like: their clothes are not torn, there is no weapon, they have not been threatened, they did not scream.

Again, I remind the reader, she was thirteen years old.

On the issue of consent, Adv Kemp proceeds to question Fezekile about Charles, who Fezekile also says raped her when she was still a child in exile.

'So he raped you in all senses of the word, it was without your consent?'

'That is correct, yes.'

'We are not talking now about what the age of consent is, I am simply asking you as a matter of fact?'

I am not surprised that there was a long pause from Fezekile. When a formidable advocate says '[w]e are not talking now about what the age of consent is', it is baffling – when Fezekile had tried to raise this point, she was told not to worry about the legal definition of the age of consent but rather to focus on whether she had consented or not. Throughout, she has been asked to account for the actions of adult men, and how she consented to them as a child.

She then gathers her thoughts and says, 'I at this point do not remember exactly what happened and between then and now I always say it was a rape, so it is hard for me to say what part of it am I saying it is rape because he did not ask me, when I say it is rape, because I was 13.'

'Just help me, at the time you knew that whether you gave consent or not it would still be rape?'

'At that particular time, no.'

Adv Kemp then asks Fezekile whether it is correct that she accused both Charles and Godfrey of raping her. After the incident with Charles, a committee of aunties was set up to look into the issue. Fezekile says that she did not actually lay any charges against Godfrey, but rather, when asked whether anybody else had done to her what Charles had done, she then mentioned Godfrey. (The uncle whose girlfriend beat her up with a big spoon. So severe was the beating that the spoon broke.)

Fezekile says she could not have laid a charge because she was thirteen and would not have known where to go. It is the committee of aunties in exile and what she described as 'some kangaroo ANC court case' that took place and found the two guilty of rape.

Adv Kemp then puts it to Fezekile that she had, in fact, told the committee at the ANC hearing that 'the sex was with [her] consent': 'Ms Kuzwayo, you in fact told the committee that those two were boyfriends of yours?'

'That is not true.'

When I asked Fezekile about this she became upset, asking rhetorically, 'Can you believe it? At thirteen, I was so powerful and confident that I pursued grown comrades. Can you believe this was accepted? Both of them were my boyfriends and they each knew about the other?'

'*Ja*, one fool at a time indeed.'

We laughed, for a moment. But she was truly traumatised by these childhood experiences and how they were presented in court.

Adv Kemp tells the court that one of the aunties, Aunt Nomswakazi, has told the defence that when the aunties questioned Fezekile, she had said that Charles and Godfrey were her boyfriends. At thirteen, she was bold enough to tell adults that she had two adult boyfriends and had had consensual sex with them? The point that Adv Kemp wished to make was that the two had not been found guilty of rape. They had also not been found guilty of having sex with her without consent – not that there is a difference between rape and having sex with a minor, as a minor cannot consent – but rather, they had been punished because they had had consensual sex with a child.

'Ms Kuzwayo may I say to you, you are wrong as well. They were both found guilty of having sex with a young child and they were both I think docked six months of their allowances that they received over there and the reason for that punishment was because it was found that they did not have sex with you without your consent and that was after you had told that they were your boyfriends and that this was not without consent.'

So, Kemp is arguing that the two men were found not guilty of rape, but of having had consensual sex with a child. If ever there was a scenario that misses the nuances and dynamics of power relations, grooming and predatory behaviour, this is it. There is absolutely no grasp of what it means for a grown man to creep up on a child and not recognise that this child does not have the agency and maturity to be an equal partner – that her 'consent' has no value because she is a child. That, even if she had said yes, it still constituted a violation. But Adv Kemp was interested in contestable facts – not the exercise of male, adult power over a child.

The court then hears more details about the 'trial' by committee and Fezekile's reaction to it from Fezekile's diary, in which she had written:

> He is being punished or not, did not matter to me. I could not have cared less. I was happy about the process having gone as far as him being found guilty … Aunt Promise and Nomswakazi sat me down. Then I was happy that after all the failed attempts on my part my mother finally knew about it. The best part of it all was that they all told me that I have done nothing wrong. That it has all been his fault, that they love me and I was going to be fine … I shall one day have to sit down with Aunt Promise and perhaps Aunt Nomswakazi if I can find her and let them tell me their side of the story.

All I can extrapolate from this diary entry is that Fezekile was relieved that the two men were punished.

The incident with Mashaya is even stranger – if Fezekile had consented, why did she point a gun at him?

'Did you at some stage before the sex point a gun at him?'

'I remember a gun in the room. I honestly sitting here do not remember what exactly happened, but I remember the gun and I remember, I do not know whether I actually took it but I know that I definitely thought about it, and I remember that I actually did not know how to use it, that I was aware that I did not know how to use it.'

Adv Kemp then moves on to other questions and the gun theme is abandoned. At this point, it is difficult to make the connection between her 'consenting' and then pointing a gun at him. It was not put to her that the gun story was untrue; the story was not disputed.

The gun incident was so dramatic and bizarre that I had to ask her about it.

'I was just enraged. I just had this blinding rage. I was sick of all this, all of it, so I grabbed the gun,' she told me.

'Sick of what?'

'Men, marking themselves on my body.'

'Did you expect it to come up at the trial?'

'No, no, I mean it was so long ago and oh dear, I don't know what it had to do with anything. Maybe they were trying to say I am crazy.' She laughed.

While Godfrey's girlfriend was beating Fezekile after the incident with Mashaya, Godfrey came to the door of the locked room and said, '*Kwanele*. (Enough now.)' His girlfriend ignored him; Godfrey left. Fez wrote in her diary: 'That was the only time that he said anything and he did not even try to do anything else when she ignored him. I heard the door closed. I think he left the house.'

From this entry, Adv Kemp asks, 'Does that not indicate resentment towards Godfrey for not interfering [intervening]?'

Fezekile answers that she had not felt resentful at all and makes a valid point – that she wrote about the incident long after it had happened, and was asked by the aunties whether Godfrey had done anything to help. Her response was solicited, not something she intuitively felt and expressed.

Adv Kemp's question plants the seed of motive – that so resentful was Fezekile about Godfrey's complacency and disengagement that she would go as far as making false rape accusations against him. But we had just heard Adv Kemp challenging Fezekile that she had admitted to consensual sex and that Godfrey had been her boyfriend. So, the argument about feeling resentful does not make sense if it is being put to her that she consented and was publicly acknowledging Godfrey to be her boyfriend. Also, if the accusation against her or the evidence presented to the court was that she had a habit of falsely accusing men of rape, then why was it put to her that she had admitted to being in a relationship with both these men – which nullifies the rape accusation? It did not make sense to be accused of making false rape claims, yet also accused of, or of admitting to, being in relationships with the men.

She could not have known that this chapter in her life would be aired in court and that she would have to account for the veracity of her claims. If she had told the aunties – at age thirteen – that she had had a romantic relationship with these grown men, why would she write, almost two decades later, in her private pages that they had raped her? If the narrative of false claims is to be sustained, it would have been more plausible, I reckon, had she falsely accused them of rape at the ANC tribunal – and then, in her private pages, which she could not imagine would be presented in court, admitted that she had lied. It should have been the other way around: the 'false rape claim' at the hearing, and the truth in her diary.

And then, something so odd and bizarre arose that it defied logic and family norms. According to Adv Kemp, those testifying at the ANC tribunal all those years ago – particularly Auntie Nomswakazi – were willing to testify that Fezekile's mother 'was not very concerned about these allegations especially as far as Godfrey was concerned'. The aunties allege that, at the time, Beauty had said that, if a sexual relationship between Fezekile and Godfrey was what they both wanted, then it was okay.

A mother is alleged to have been happy with a sexual relationship between her child and an adult male? Yes, these things happen in dysfunctional families and often are influenced by poverty where, tragically, parents sell their children for food and money. But Beauty is accused of putting a stamp of approval on this relationship for no reason whatsoever. It is also odd that she would be comfortable being in the same room as Godfrey and Fezekile if she perceived what was happening between them to be of a romantic and sexual nature. Not only was she alleged to have been 'okay' with this relationship, but also to have been 'okay' with them doing it right in front of her?

Fezekile disputes the version put to the court and says, 'I remember my mother to be totally devastated by what had happened.' This seems a most likely reaction by a mother, but, in court, Beauty was presented as an unusually laissez-faire mother.

'Pertaining to your mother's attitude at the hearing? Can you recall anything like that?'

'The only thing I remember was Godfrey saying something to the effect that I deserved what he did to me and my mother allowed me to walk around the house, I do not remember whether it was half naked or naked, but basically that I had it coming because my mother allowed me to, and I very clearly remember my mother saying that he had no right to do it and even if, she actually said verbatim even if I was a prostitute he would not have the right to rape me.'

For Fezekile, walking around naked had no sexual meaning. She simply felt comfortable being at home, in the nude.

Kemp then draws attention to, and questions Fezekile about, a paragraph in 'her book' that confirms Fezekile's stance about her mother's reaction, and not the stance that Beauty accepted a sexual relationship between her daughter and Godfrey. Fezekile had, again, written these words many years ago, when she would have had no clue that the matter would ever be brought up in court: 'The fact that some of the men in that room might have, like him, believed that he was not wrong, that it was not rape, that my mother had given me to him did not matter'.

I suspect that, here, there was a language challenge, with English being both Adv Kemp's and Fezekile's second language. It is clear in the build-up to this paragraph being brought to the attention of the court and what happens next that Kemp took the words 'that my mother had given me to him did not matter' as a statement separate from the rest of the paragraph. Fezekile meant that the fact that some of the men in that room may have believed, as Godfrey did, that her mother had given her to him did not matter. She is emphatically saying that it does not matter that they believed her mother had given her to him – *not* that it did not matter *because* her mother had given her to him.

This is where the language and interpretation of what constitutes sexual violence is problematic. Even if Beauty had 'given her daughter' to Godfrey, sex with Fezekile still constitutes rape and reflects moral decay on the part of the grown men who abused her. It also reflects a deeply patriarchal and predatory mindset – one in which a child's body is seen as a commodity to be given to a man, something to which he is entitled. It is also worth pointing out that a child is no less deserving of justice if his or her parents are complicit in his or her abuse.

'I just want on this issue to put to you that the witness will say your mother's attitude was if it was consensual that was in order,' Adv Kemp stated.

'That is not true,' Fezekile responded.

The theme of the childhood experiences ends with Adv Kemp saying, 'I must say to you that I want to put it to you that in respect of [Mashaya], Godfrey and Charles that you accused each of them in two cases of having raped you, and in the other case of attempting to rape you whilst in all those three instances what happened took place with your consent.' This assertion is, for me, a clear indication of hostility directed at women and children who come to the courts for succour. It is as clear an indication as any that, in that courtroom, those presiding over the process had lost a sense of what destroys. The language is grotesque, abusive and disempowering, with Adv Kemp bluntly accusing her of being a willing player in specific incidents involving three adult males. He makes no provision

for the mind of a child; if we close our eyes and think of the five-, twelve-
and thirteen-year-olds that we know, how much power do they really have
over men in their twenties and thirties?

The focus in this part of the trial on Fezekile as a five-, twelve- and
thirteen-year-old should make us demand that the men involved look
at themselves and ask, 'What kind of human being am I? What does it
say about me that I afford myself the right to devour a child?' Fezekile's
alleged conduct is irrelevant; masculinity that perceives itself as the
victim of a child's seduction should recoil at its own moral and ethical
paucity. Society should do its own introspection and ask why it was,
and is, eager to accept the version of a man who can state, in a court of
law, that he had consensual sex with a child. Our societal mores have
enabled this.

It is shameful.

The trial offers us an opportunity to broaden the parameters of the
meaning of consent. Firstly, there are many ways of saying no. And
Fezekile did, in many ways, say no. Secondly, consent must encompass
the relationship between the one who seeks consent and the one from
whom consent is sought. A few years ago, I broke down on the radio
over the gang rape of a mentally ill young woman. The young men in
her neighbourhood took advantage of her. One of them filmed her. She
can be heard pleading with one of them to be gentle. She does not tell
him to stop, but asks him not to hurt her. She took the R2 that was given
to her afterwards. Is that consent?

What is the psychology behind the consent of one who does not hold
equal status in the relationship, and what does it say about the man who
wields power and who may not abduct, hit or tie a woman down, but
uses his stature to subdue her emotionally and mentally? Does the word
'consent' take these nuances into consideration? Are the laws and institutions that administer the law attuned to these complexities?

The fact of the matter remains, however, that the court viewed some aspects of Fezekile's testimony in a critical light, and stated that it did not set out to discredit Fezekile. In his judgment, Judge van der Merwe states the following: 'The evidence concerning Godfrey and Charles was led, not to reflect on the complainant's bad sexual history or sexual experiences, but merely to indicate that she was prone, at a young age already, to make allegations of rape when no rape took place.' He continues that further evidence was 'not led to show that the complainant was of loose morals. The evidence was led to show that the complainant was inclined to falsely accuse men of having raped or attempted to rape her'; he found that the childhood incidents that Fezekile experienced were not rape.

· · ·

Khethani Mbatha arrived in Johannesburg from rural KwaZulu-Natal in 1989. She, like countless others, had come to the City of Gold to find work. She lived in a male hostel in Khumalo Street. The creators of these hostels went home every night to their wives and children. But, in the city, black men were ordered to live alone. Creating draconian and unreasonable laws is the surest way to ensure that they are not obeyed. At this particular hostel, the Induna agreed that there should be a women's room. Khethani shared this room with several people.

The hostels were mainly inhabited by Zulu men, who were culturally and politically aligned to the Inkatha Freedom Party (IFP), a party found to have been sponsored by the apartheid government to unleash what was macabrely known as 'black-on-black' violence. The men who inhabited the hostels of the townships may have been living in a mixed, urban environment, but their tribal links ran deep.

People who came from the direction of Natalspruit were thought to be from the township, and thus belonging to the ANC. A decree was issued that anyone who was seen walking from that direction must be killed. Those from Thokoza could not travel to Natalspruit either.

It was horrific, Khethani says. 'Many people were burnt, stabbed and shot.'

Early one evening, she saw a woman limping towards the hostel from the Natalspruit side. She had come to consult Ndwanda, a traditional healer residing in the hostel's block K.

'Her leg was dark and swollen. She was sick and desperate.'

The woman asked Khethani for directions. Instead of leading her to the healer, Khethani chastised her for arriving at the hostel, especially so late in the day: 'You will be killed here, you have to get out of here.'

A group of men was standing nearby, eavesdropping on their conversation.

She called Nomusa, another woman from the women's room at the hostel. The two of them hurriedly tried to get the woman, whose name she cannot remember, out of the hostel.

'We could not even take her to a nearby hospital. It was not safe there either.'

They tried to help her find a back route. One of the men called Khethani by name and asked her who the limping young woman was and where they were going.

'I told them she is my relative, she'd come to visit and we were walking her to the taxi rank.' She had no sense of any danger and continued walking.

'As we walked, a group of men was following us and the gap between us was getting shorter. I am not sure if it was the same group of men who had been standing at the corner and had spoken to me. I am not sure of that.'

Once the young woman had safely crossed the border into Thokoza, Nomusa and Khethani turned back, but were accosted by the group of men on Ndlovunyana Street. Nomusa managed to escape. They did not chase after her, although they could have. There were five of them. They circled Khethani and dragged her to the back of Mkhathizwe High School, tore her clothes off and took turns to rape her.

'I did not cry, I did not scream, I could not. I watched. I just watched as five men, five men, just took their turn, playing on my body.'

'Playing on your body?'

'Yes, like a soccer ball, being kicked around, passed from one person to the other. It was like that, my body became a soccer ball. I just lay on my back. You know when someone gets raped, you lie on your back.'

The last of the five men pulled out a huge knife.

'It still did not occur to me to cry or scream. I just accepted that it was my time.'

One of the men discouraged him from stabbing and killing her, saying, 'Leave her, she poses no threat. She does not know us.' And, 'Na ye ho wa kwaZulu. Ho wa ka Gatsha naye. (She is also from the Zulu tribe. She is also Gatsha's follower.)'

Khethani says the men also spoke isiZulu – not the pure version from KwaZulu-Natal, but the urban, township kind. They took her as one of their own, yet violated her because, she believes, she had assisted the enemy. A while later, four of them left, but one remained and repeatedly raped her for what felt like an eternity.

'That pain, the pain, the humiliation of being penetrated by a man who is not yours. Even now, as I speak to you, it is like this is happening to me again.' She puts her face in her hands and cries.

Afterwards, Khethani was the one limping. It was dark; bizarrely, her violator, the one who had come close to stabbing and killing her, saw fit to walk her home, for her safety. If there had been a trial, I am certain the defence would have claimed they were lovers, that he posed no danger to her. Why else would he care enough to walk her home, and why did she accept the offer?

She washed herself and slept.

For years, she says, she did not cry, did not speak, did not tell anyone. There was no point. She did not know these men and she was a woman against all five of them. There would be no victory for her. More than two decades later, she says she battles to sleep. She struggles to feel clean.

She did not see Nomusa that evening. The next morning, Nomusa asked her what had happened.

'You left me with criminals, that is what happened.'

Without asking for details, Nomusa knew what had happened. It was not difficult to guess; it is generally what happened to women alone with violent men. Nomusa advised her to never ever mention it to anyone, ever: 'Abantu ba zo ku thuka ngayo lento. (People will use this to insult you.)' And so, the burden of her silence began.

With the township under siege, they could not access the hospital or clinic. Nomusa took Khethani to a mobile clinic for some treatment.

'But my child this is a wound, it is a wound that will never heal. My child does not know, my sister, this haunts me.'

When she is triggered and her mind wanders to that horrible evening, Khethani shuts down. She locks her door and cries for days.

'I find men revolting. A male person to me spells danger.' She pauses. 'I wish they had killed me.' She cries again. 'I was lucky not to get HIV. Even now, I test obsessively, just to check that they did not leave me with anything. After ruining my soul, you see, what else, what else?'

'Why do you think this happened to you? I mean, now, do you think something like that could happen?'

'Of course it could happen again, it is just something that men do

and those who don't do it, don't do anything to stop their sons and friends from doing it. But now, if it happened, it would not be for the same reasons as before.'

Khethani is not educated, but life and the trauma of being a woman have opened her eyes in ways that a formal education could not have done. She sees an irrevocable link between rape and politics.

'Were it not for the war, for the political battle of that time, I would not have been raped in that way. It is hard to explain. There is always rape in society but that kind of rape that I experienced, that so many women experienced here in Thokoza, it was about politics. But even now, we women in South Africa are regarded as things to be raped.'

And, finally: 'I will die with this wound.'

Of all the women I interviewed in my research about their rape experiences, only one of them had screamed – from pain, rather than as a cry for help.

Like many women in her terrible position, Khethani froze. Freezing is a legitimate and common reaction to trauma, as argued by the psychologist called by the prosecution, Dr Merle Friedman. But the grey areas that make trauma such a complex and fluid phenomenon are often not accommodated in the austere and limited environment that is the courtroom. Like all rigidly masculine and restrictive environments, it presents rational thought as superior to emotional reaction. It also pits the two spheres of being against each other, with emotional reaction being perceived as feminine, inferior and less valid.

Adv Kemp asks Dr Friedman, 'Doctor let me put it to you this way. Where are the statistics that show that the majority of women just freeze? Are there statistics?'

'Yes of course there are.'

'That say the majority of women freeze?'

'Yes and certainly my experience is that.' She goes on to quote HS Bracha:[22] 'Based on recent literature, freeze, flight, fight, fright, faint provides a more complete description of the human acute stress response sequence than current descriptions.'

Adv Kemp then says, 'I have no problem with that statement. Can I just ask you did he leave out shouting for help because it did not start with an F?'

Adv Kemp may have been saying this in jest, trying to create a light moment, or he may very well have been mocking and pouring scorn on this psychology. Dr Friedman did not find it funny: 'I do not think that that comment really requires an answer.'

'No it does in a sense because what I am saying to you obviously one of the things that one has to consider is I think that in most cases of human trauma one of the first reaction if it is at all possible is to call for help?'

Dr Friedman stands her ground: 'I am the trauma specialist and I know that the answer is not so. So the reality is that what, and there are many examples of how the thing that we would regard as a normal response does not happen. So you and I sitting here might expect that somebody would call for help and in a traumatic event where they are completely overwhelmed they cannot.'

'I do not dispute and I do not take issue with you that there may be cases, may be a number of cases where the response to what you call a traumatic event or a threatening traumatic event would be to freeze. That is not the point. The issue in this court really is whether the complainant falls in that category and that is why I am asking you these questions.'

'My response to that is that, in the light of her early experiences and the fact that she tends to numb out and dissociate under extreme stress, it is most likely and virtually predictable that she would not call out and that she would freeze.'

Adv Kemp then masterfully argues that, during Fezekile's previous rapes, she had reacted: she asked Godfrey to stop, and pointed a gun at Mashaya. So, 'clearly', she is capable of fighting back, as it were, and it does not follow that she would have frozen at Forest Town.

This part of the trial is not insignificant. It is a further reflection of machismo, a masculinity that cannot be vulnerable. It is inconceivable, in this socially constructed masculinity, for the past to haunt one, for an experience to overwhelm and disempower one. Masculinity does not have a tradition of making itself vulnerable, of being affected by past events. Its pillars are rational thought (or so it claims); it regards rational thought and emotion as mutually exclusive. Looking at Fezekile's reaction through this prism of masculinity, her reaction does not make sense. A court of law is intimidating. In a trial dominated by males – who, by virtue of their gender, may not be acutely attuned to the vagaries of trauma and vulnerability – Fezekile was othered.

'I just had an out-of-body experience,' she told me. 'I just did and I don't know how else one describes that. It is what happened.'

'We have spoken a lot about your happy places, your tuning out from reality and going to your happy places. Are you describing something similar?' I probed.

'I did freeze, I did tune out but I can't exactly say I went to my happy places. In happy places I see friends, the ocean, children. I did not shut my mind down and travel to a happy place. I just froze and left that room, maybe I floated, I don't know, I just left.'

I don't see society's construct of masculinity – and certainly how masculinity plays out in a violent society – as able to grasp these legitimate experiences.

. . .

Fezekile told me that the hardest part of the trial, the most humiliating, was when her sexual history was revealed. 'I remember now, I remember wishing it would all end. I remember just wanting to be in my bed. But I did not feel that I had done anything wrong in being a sexually active adult,' she recalled.

The defence had successfully applied for her sexual history to be interrogated because she had accused other men of rape before. The state did not oppose this; the ruling was that only those experiences pertaining to alleged false accusation could be brought, but her entire sexual history, including relationships that did not fall into this category, was laid bare.

It was unprecedented, a top judge tells me. An advocate says, 'Kemp got away with a lot. He rightly persuaded the court that some aspect of her sexual history was relevant. But then he went beyond the parameters and the judge let him get away with it.' Another senior advocate says he finds it interesting that this judgment has not been referred to in any trial subsequently and that, in ten years, no one is invoking or quoting from it: 'That is how astounding the judgment was.'

Fezekile was questioned about everything, including the men with whom she admitted to having consensual sex. I battle to see why these sexual encounters were relevant. So clumsy was this chapter of the trial that she even had to account to the whole world for all the kisses and blow jobs she'd performed.

One such encounter was with a person referred to in court as Z, a sexual relationship that Fezekile did not deny and was thus not relevant to the proceedings as per the court ruling. In addition, much was made about the frequency with which Fezekile had sex. She had claimed far less than what was put to her, but the defence argued that she had a very active sex life. This, too, is designed to send a particular message about a victim of rape: that she is a slut, a woman of questionable morals and

118

virtue. If she had never accused these specific men of rape, why did it matter how often she had sex? Surely the issue before court was the rape accusation and, relevant to that, whatever is deemed to be a previous false rape accusation? But there she was, in the dock, having to recall and account for every penis she had touched and mouth she had kissed.

Adv Kemp: 'So did you stop in 1996 to have sex with Z?'

'Yes.'

'And from 1999 to the middle of 2004 with how many people did you have consensual sex?'

'I remember the male that I had sex with in 2004. You said up to when, sorry?'

'Up to the middle of 2004 because you testified that is the last time that you had sex before the events in question.'

'Any sex?'

'Yes, consensual sex with a male.'

'With a male?'

'Yes.'

'Maybe I will remember later, I cannot really you know, time frames and things, I cannot remember now. I cannot think of someone.'

I can just imagine the effect of this admission from Fez – that she cannot really remember. In this world of skewed power relations and demands that women be pure and virtuous, her not remembering could mean only one thing: that she was a slut. In this world, women are supposed to remember every kiss, every touch, every encounter with a man, because such encounters are meant to be so few and so precious. There is an unwritten rule that women are supposed to have sex with one man and that men, of course, can fuck whoever they want, whenever they want, and just as quickly move to another conquest without ever having to account for their conduct. In addition, society does not expect women to have meaningless, forgettable sex with equally forgettable males. This is why Fezekile's response was always going to receive a hostile reception from a hostile society.

Kemp continues, 'Are you still thinking or can I ask you a question?'

'You can carry on.'

'Is not the answer simple from what you told me, is it not four? I thought you said to me you had consensual sex with five male people in your life. Was I right as far as that is concerned?'

'That number was just, I just meant to say less than five, number one, but also if you want me to include non-penetrative sex then I can remember two people, two men, that was non-penetrative.'

This exchange continues with another name being introduced to the proceedings; a man called Mashaya, with whom Fez had had consensual sex. Here the debate centres around frequency and location: whether the sex happened in Zimbabwe or Zambia.

'And in Zimbabwe what is your answer to that maybe?'

'There was some form of sex it may – it is very possible – that it was penetrative on that one occasion in some flat in Zimbabwe yes.'

She is then asked to recall and write down the names of other men with whom she has had consensual sex. The next question – 'Did you know them well?' – goes unanswered, initially.

'Are you thinking, is it so difficult to tell whether you knew them well?'

'I knew them,' she responds

'You knew them?'

'Yes.'

'Did you know them well that was the question?'

'I knew them is enough I think.'

Here, I read, women who have sex with men whom they do not 'know well' are loose and have no credibility. Why does it matter how well she knew them if the point is that the sex was consensual and she admits to it?

They return once again to the number of sexual partners she has had in her lifetime.

'Let us do it systematically it seems to be the only way. In your entire life, forget the rapes that you have described in those documents, just tell us in your entire life how may men had you had non-penetrative sex, but before you do that what I want you to tell the court is what do you regard as non-penetrative sex?'

'A penis not entering my vagina or any other part of my body or my mouth or anything, that is not penetrative.'

'But I suppose kissing would not qualify?'

'Kissing would not qualify as?'

'Non-penetrative sex?'

'It is non-penetrative because I am talking about the penis.'

'Ms Kuzwayo when you say that you had only non-penetrative sex with two men because you were talking your entire life consensually five, we have now discovered that two of them were non-penetrative sex, if you only kissed two males in your life.'

Here it seems they are going around in circles. The court intervenes: 'I think you are at different angles now because she in that answer had made reference to a penis, I do not know whether that is a kiss on the penis or what I do not know, I am not trying to be funny; the point is you immediately brought the penis into the picture, so if you can just describe that to us and I know it is difficult and I want to get it over and done with as soon as possible, can you just explain what you meant by that?'

'Okay, let me try and explain,' Fezekile responds. The court hands over to Adv Kemp once again, and Fezekile continues, 'All right. I have had sex with not more than five men, consensual sex, penetrative or not, and I have kissed all five of them.'

Kemp, noting the sting in Fezekile's words, says, 'So that was a clever point at my expense Ms Kuzwayo, I concede that, now tell me of the five did you have penetrative sex with any of the five?'

For a woman who is accused of herself falsely accusing men of rape, it seems strange that she is on trial for every sexual encounter she has had, including those to which she consented. The defence does not pursue this point further, but a clear picture has emerged: a picture of a wanton woman who has regular sex with men she does not know well.

She was also questioned about how she acquired HIV, with the advocate almost chastising her for having unprotected sex and contracting the virus. Ironic, given that the man in the dock had *knowingly* had sex with an HIV-positive Fezekile.

'How did you feel about your sexual history being laid bare like that? Did you expect that to happen?' I asked.

'I did not go into that trial with expectations, to be honest. I didn't. I just wanted to fight for myself.'

'But you must have considered a lot of things, anticipated the trial, how it would be conducted, what you would be asked ...'

'I did not really reflect much on that. For a long time, I kept thinking, what was he thinking, what made him do it? What made him think he could get away with it?'

'In fact, you told Kimmy that there must be something in your panties that made him do it.'

'Yes.'

'You were interrogated about that at the trial. My impressions were that the defence had misunderstood what you meant by that ...?'

'They totally misunderstood me. What do you think I meant?'

'I thought you meant it as a self-deprecating comment, really. That what is so wrong about you, what is it about your body that seems to attract that kind of abuse, since you have experienced this before?'

'*Yebo dade.* That is exactly right. I thought there was something wrong with my body that this keeps happening. But I was questioned as if I was boasting about something in my panties.'

'So let's go back to your sexual history and how you did not expect that to come up in court ...'

'I cannot say I was or was not expecting it. As I said, dear, I did not pause to think about it, I did not think it was something to be embarrassed about, or something wrong so I could not have feared it coming up in a bad way.'

'But you told me previously that the hardest part of the trial was the vilification and the sexual history?'

'Oh, did I? *Ja*, maybe, but every day there was something new, so today, this was hard, tomorrow a different thing would be hard, difficult, you know ... I guess what I mean is that I had not prepared for that. I had not expected my sexual history to feature so prominently. And remember the recordings that were done during my consultation with Charin [de Beer]. I did not expect those conversations to come up.'

'But it did come out. There was a picture painted of you ... an impression created of you ...'

'*Ja*, I know. It was wrong.'

'Were you hurt, embarrassed?'

Fezekile does not remember how she felt about this as it was unfolding. At that time, she does not remember this aspect being overwhelming. Only later, when she thought about it, did she realise that she had been set up for profound humiliation. At that point, there had been so many betrayals, so many people who had tried to bully her, so many friends lost, that it was hard to pick which battle was hardest. But this line of questioning must have taken a toll on her because, after being interrogated about her sexual history, she conceded, not for the first time, consensual sex with two other men and ended with,

'I am sorry I am actually very tired now, I really am exhausted.'

The court was adjourned until the next day.

. . .

Beauty's strength was tested during the trial. She seemed to handle questioning about her relationship with her daughter, her friendship with Zuma, life in exile, and so on with equanimity, but unravelled – as any mother would – when it was implied that she had given permission for her twelve-year-old daughter to have sex with a grown comrade, then a thirty-one-year-old man.

Throughout her testimony, Beauty had been softly spoken, yet clear. But when it was put to her that she approved of her daughter getting into bed with a grown man, she almost lost her mind. Referring to that incident from the 1980s, the defence advocate asked, 'On my instructions Madam at that hearing your daughter recanted the allegation of rape and suggested, or told them that there was consensual sex. Do you remember anything about that?'

She responded: 'If I may disagree with that. As far as I know there was no consent.'

The incredulity did not stop there. Counsel continued: 'Now there is also a suggestion that you would allow your daughter to sleep with Godfrey in his bed.'

Even before I met MaKuzwayo, my instincts rejected the idea that a mother would agree to her twelve-year-old girl sleeping and having sex with a grown man. Even when this does happen, it is regarded as abuse and often occurs in exchange for money because the parents are poor, for example, and have no means of supporting themselves. Here, it was being suggested that Beauty gave her daughter away for no reason at all.

Even if she had agreed to this sordid arrangement, it would still constitute sexual abuse of a minor. The defence seemed to suggest that when a mother 'agrees' to her daughter sharing a bed with a grown man, it does not constitute abuse.

I argue that even if Fezekile herself had agreed to this, she would still fit the profile of an abused little girl who had, perhaps, been groomed by the adult Godfrey. She was a child: how could she be expected to have the faculties to make responsible decisions about sex and relationships? Again, the twelve-year-old girl was required to account for her actions, while the adult male who should have known better was not expected to account for his. No one asked why he did not just cuddle Fezekile like a father would a daughter – why her presence in his bed meant he had to penetrate her. Could he not just leave her alone? Is that how weak menfolk are? Can they not just lie in a bed with a child, a minor?

I think about all the times I shared a bed with my father when my mother, a nurse, was on night duty. I was between the ages of six and eight. I slept soundly and, when the night was too long and dark, I cuddled up to my father. Sometimes he put his big, protective arm around me. Sometimes, I had my leg over his body, my torso and face on his body, breathing him in as I slept. I woke up in one peace the next morning, and the next.

We grew up with my mother's youngest brother, Jabanxa, living with us for a few years in Soweto. I was a little girl. He walked us to school, looked after us when our parents were away. My brother loved to play in the streets so I was often at home, alone with Jabanxa. I'd fall asleep on the couch with my head on his lap. We did not have a bathroom, so we bathed over a big enamel dish in the one bedroom we had. I'd call his name when I was struggling to pull my clothes over my head. I did not even pause to think about what it meant to be naked in my uncle's presence. There was no name for it, and he certainly got on with things without any discomfort.

I was his niece. It was right to feel safe in his presence. And he was right not to interpret my 'actions' in any way other than him being a caring uncle.

What was the defence saying about men? That they just could not leave little girls alone? Godfrey may have been punished in a clumsy, inadequate way, but there is no doubt that, in this encounter, the victim was Fezekile. Charges were not laid with the Zambian police because the ANC in exile sorted out its own problems, the court heard. Fezekile had gone to the bed of a man who was minding his own business, and Beauty took the blame. She took strong exception to this. Her dignified veneer cracked.

When Adv Brauns put it to her that 'she would allow' Fezekile to occupy Godfrey's bed, she answered, 'That is an insult to me, that is how I view it.'

'That never happened you say?'

'It did not happen.'

'If Godfrey says that when he testifies ...'

'It is an insult, I disagree. I would not have, even now old as she is, I would not just say to any man sleep with my child. I am not talking about a 13-year-old. It is an insult to me, whoever says that. That is an insult, it is an insult.'

'Well Godfrey will say it Madam.'

Men like Zuma, who claim to adhere to culture and tradition, know that this culture does not allow for mothers to give their daughters away. Yet he sat there, quietly, and pretended that it was possible for a mother to watch as her daughter got into bed with a grown man for sexual purposes. He knew it was improbable that a mother – an African, Zulu mother – would consent to what happened.

MaKuzwayo was right to be upset and insulted. She comes across as an old-school mom who loves God, family and church. It is unthinkable that she would agree to her daughter 'servicing' grown men. It defies logic in any language, culture, or race. Yet this was the argument put before the court, and it stuck. Fezekile was a slut. She had been one since childhood; her mother was not only comfortable with that, but also actively pushed her into men's beds for no reason; because Beauty had agreed, Godfrey did not rape young Fezeka.

Like Fezekile, Beauty was on trial.

In her testimony, Beauty continued to educate the all-male, majority-white defence team:

> The way I was brought up by my parents, both my mother and my father did not tell me or instruct me to go to bed with this one and that one. I do not know if that happens, I never do it, I do not know it. That would be insulting my parents. I would not say I am blameless, I am not an angel but I try by all means to do as they had taught me.

Much was also made about Fezekile's therapy sessions while in exile. Again, Beauty had to argue that these sessions with the psychologist and psychiatrist 'did not mean she was mentally not sound'.

Adv Brauns continued his questioning: 'Is it correct that there was a mental institution not far from where you lived in Zambia called Chamaima?'

'Yes.'

'Did your daughter attend sessions at that hospital? [...] If there was evidence that she attended therapy sessions at this mental institution in Zambia, you would not dispute them would you?'

The question implies that this is something Beauty wished to hide.

She didn't. She admitted to her daughter being in therapy in Zimbabwe – she just could not remember whether the same had happened in Zambia. All this was close to two decades ago; the substance of it she did not dispute, but she had forgotten the intricate details.

The purpose of this was obviously to prove that Fezekile was mad.

I have already stated that there was only one female in the legal team. In this trial, the demographics of each legal team and of the judge are not insignificant. For the state, there was one white Afrikaans female (Adv de Beer), one white Afrikaans male (Adv Broodryk SC) and one black male (Adv Nengovhela). For the defence, there were two white Afrikaans males (Adv Kemp SC and Adv Brauns SC), and one black male (Adv Mbonga). And the judge, of course, was another Afrikaans man (Judge Willem van der Merwe).

This is South Africa, with its plurality of voices and histories. Group identity and affiliation matters in a country where black people and women have been marginalised. It matters in a country where white people, in particular, have never had to navigate black cultures and live side by side with them; it matters in a country where gender-based discrimination is rife. In that court, society's constructed power relations were at play. The demographic of the courtroom does not suggest that the legal team was incapable of running proceedings according to the law. What it means is that its members' grasp of Fezekile and Zuma's language and cultural practices was not nuanced.

The association of psychological or psychiatric therapy with 'madness' or 'instability' is a masculine outlook. From the masculine perspective, it demonstrates weakness. It was left to her mother to explain the obvious.

'What was wrong with your daughter?'

I thought being raped at age five, twelve and thirteen was a good start, but Beauty answered softly:

After her father's death she experienced hallucinations and night-mares. She had a pain on her middle, or her belly button and she started wetting her bed, a thing she had outgrown even before she turned 18 months. According to the hospital there was nothing wrong with her stomach. She was then given tablets which were actually taken by mad people and that aggravated her condition.

Beauty went on to tell the court, without any pressure, that Fezekile's nightmares and hallucinations became worse, then also got better, after she saw a psychologist.

The defence seemed particularly interested in the fact that these sessions with the psychologist continued into Fezekile's adulthood, 'to the present day'. This suggests that depression, trauma and their concomitant behaviour have a sell-by date: that what happens to us in childhood or at any stage of our lives should have no bearing on our present and, if and when it does, it is something to interrogate and present as negative. It is not clear when, exactly, Fez was supposed to 'get over' her childhood rapes, her father's death and her unsettled life. The court did not seem to appreciate the enormity of these events.

But Beauty did:

> You see according to me to experience so many difficulties, being raped at the age of five, the age of 12, 13, having your father dying in a tragic motor accident [...], seeing your comrades die, your uncles die in exile, attacked and die and then you finally come home, you do not have a matric certificate, you do not qualify because you have got an O level which does not tie in with a South African matric, you cannot get to university, you try to write your exams and you fail because you do not know Afrikaans, the subjects are different and finally you get into (indistinct) the entry programme,

you qualify and then only to find that after seven years of study, you are starting to now settle and then you find that you are HIV positive. You are given tablets which make you a zombi [*sic*], you end up not being able to study and you fail your assignments and the university expels you and all that. Actually I think I also need a psychologist but I have been resisting because we did not grow up like that, so I believe she needs a psychologist. We are all supposed to undergo a psychologist when we came back from exile because of the traumas that we experienced in exile.

Her answer speaks to the unresolved trauma for which the new South Africa appears to have no appetite.

· · ·

It was widely reported that Zuma saw himself as a victim during his trial. He and his supporters claimed that Fezekile had been set up as a honeytrap to scupper his political aspirations, and that Ronnie Kasrils was central to this plot, allegations for which Kasrils would go on to sue Kebby Maphatsoe of the MK Military Veterans Association (MKMVA) in 2016.

Dr Jonathan Shay, an American doctor and clinical psychiatrist involved in the care of military veterans, provides fascinating interpretive tools in his analysis of moral injury and victimhood. What is fascinating about Zuma's conduct is that it displays an aspect of moral injury in as far as it demonstrates how those who benefit the most after conflict, and become heroes who correct the wrongs of society, can live their lives believing that they are victims and that they are beyond reproach because of their previous good deeds. When they are censured for their behaviour, they do not entertain the thought that they may have acted wrongly, unethically – immorally, even. They are trapped in a perpetual state of victimhood and this sense that they are under siege results in moral injury.

Ronnie Kasrils' 'role' in the Khwezi affair is strange, and made up of odd accidents of history. He was Judson Kuzwayo's comrade. He remembers meeting Fezekile as a charming little girl. He remembers time spent with Zuma and Judson, with little Fezeka in tow. They would pick her up, tickle her and treat her how any grown, sensible man would treat his friend's little girl. I have also mentioned that Kimmy's father was a senior MK member and a trusted comrade of Zuma and Kasrils.

Kasrils' path, and those of the two young women, would cross. He was the Minister for Intelligence Services at the time of the rape trial and was perceived to be in the Thabo Mbeki camp. It did not help that Kimmy, Fezekile's best friend at the time, worked in Kasrils' department. While she did not report to him directly, he was still her boss and the political head of the department. The link between Kasrils and the two young women was not strange, as many ANC members and their children work for the state.

Kasrils had never discussed Fezekile with Kimmy until one day when Fezekile needed help to raise money to pursue her studies in homeopathy. She wished to study overseas and, since she had no money of her own, she thought she could make an appeal to her father's old comrades. Fezekile emphatically denied to me that she had worked with Kasrils in a conspiracy to entrap Zuma; Kimmy finds the idea repugnant and far-fetched.

Fezekile did not, of her own volition, pick up the phone and call Kasrils. It was during discussions with Kimmy about Fezekile's plans that Kasrils' name came up as an uncle who may be able to help. Kimmy asked Kasrils if she could pass his number on to Fezekile, whom Kasrils

had not seen in decades. Fezekile also did not phone Kasrils immediately – she only called some time after Kimmy had passed on his
number.

'Hello Uncle Ronnie,' was her bright greeting – typically of Fezekile,
she greeted him as if they had never parted. They discussed her plans and
ways in which he could help. Kasrils phoned a few colleagues and comrades. So busy was he that he cannot recall whom he contacted, but he
does remember promising to speak to Tokyo Sexwale and Jacob Zuma.

He phoned Zuma and told him about Fezekile and her plight; Zuma
agreed that Kasrils could pass his number on to Fezekile.

The next call Kasrils received from Fezekile was the one in which she
broke the news: 'Uncle Zuma has raped me.' In the minds of the honeytrap
theorists, this call confirms that Kasrils was involved in a Mbeki-camp
political conspiracy to stop Zuma from becoming president.

'To think I only called Uncle Ronnie out of fear, you know, given
his position and all, I thought he could advise about security,' Fezekile
told me. The politics of the day were furthest from her mind. In fact, it
was Kimmy who advised Fezekile to phone Kasrils, but Fezekile was
reluctant, preferring Kimmy to phone because 'she knew him better'.
Kimmy's testimony confirms this:

'Did you and the complainant discuss your boss in that period we are
talking now between the 2nd and the 3rd?' Adv Kemp asked.

Kimmy responded:

> Yes, Fezeka had security concerns for herself. You know she went
> ahead and laid the charges and we kind of did not know what to do
> next given Mr Zuma's profile and we said: okay what do we do now.
> She was concerned about her safety. So she then asked me to call, just
> to ask Minister Kasrils what, you know in terms of security what can
> she do. I then called her and thought look I think it is a bit inappropriate

for me to go to him and tell him what is going on. I think maybe it is best if you discuss it with him because I still have a professional relationship to try and maintain. So she then spoke to him.

'Did it strike you during this discussion at all that if a person that you are going to phone is in the anti-Zuma camp, he is perhaps not a good choice to phone?'

Kimmy remembers this question years later with anger:

It is extraordinary. I am Fezeka's best friend, she tells me she has been raped by one of the most powerful men in South Africa, an uncle and friend of her father. Her concerns for her security were legitimate and, in our discussions, Ronnie was the most senior and connected person we both knew. So, at that time, we were supposed to not have called him and considered the pro-or anti-Zuma nonsense. Our minds were not even there. Fezeka had never ever mentioned Ronnie in that context. We had never even discussed it amongst ourselves.

She mentions again that, after Mbeki fired Zuma, she had organised a lunch to comfort Zuma. 'To now be dragged into this conspiracy thing ...'

In court, her response was, 'No I was not thinking whether a person is in the pro-Zuma camp or the anti-Zuma camp. Fezeka had concerns, Minister Kasrils was available to her to speak to and I did not see anything wrong ...'

Kasrils had been stunned to get a call from Fezekile the first time around. Months later, she and Kimmy had gone to visit him to discuss possible sponsorship for her homeopathy studies, which she was interested in pursuing in Australia. When she did phone him about a year later to report that Zuma had raped her, Kasrils froze. She had already laid a charge and Kasrils could not advise her either way. Unlike Fezekile, he was attuned to the political sensitivities of the time and was not keen to be drawn into this. At the same time, however, he did not want to appear uncaring.

He had to attend a function with President Mbeki. He found Mbeki there, and told him the news.

'Mbeki was completely floored. "Are you sure?" he asked me.'

'Well, it's what Fezeka told me.'

Mbeki, according to Kasrils, did not say another word; they never spoke about it again.

In 2016, the accusation that Kasrils had been involved in a honeytrap conspiracy returned to the public domain when he spoke on Constitution Hill at a protest against Zuma's leadership and weakening of the public institutions that are the pillars of our democracy. This was ten years after the rape trial. Kasrils and I had already started talking about my interest in writing a book about Fezekile, and he had connected me to Kimmy via email. They had both spoken to Fezekile, who had spent the last decade avoiding journalists. But Kimmy sent a message via Kasrils that Fezekile would be happy to speak to me. I remembered the conspiracy matter and hesitated; I wanted to try to get through to Fezekile using other networks. I did not want her story to be delegitimised yet again by anyone who would accuse Kasrils of being behind it.

I sought Kasrils out. He was not the only one – I contacted a lot of people who knew Fezekile and used various ways to get to her.

Kasrils made a resounding speech that criticised Zuma. As he spoke, he invoked Khwezi and spoke of her treatment and exile as a sign of Zuma's depravity. This angered Maphatsoe, one of Zuma's staunchest supporters.

History has it that Maphatsoe ran away from an MK camp, got shot and lost an arm in the process. He was not a combatant, but a camp cook. Perhaps feeding the guerrillas was an act of courage, but there are far more decorated former MK fighters and leaders who are more than qualified to lead the MKMVA. Maphatsoe insults anyone who criticises Zuma by calling them agents, CIA spies and all manner of colourful labels. He organises young men, who pose as MK veterans, to guard ANC headquarters every time there is an anti-Zuma demonstration. The real veterans, who look and sound the part, do not know who these young men and women in camouflage are. They are as mortified as the whole nation that these young people claim to have fought against apartheid in a battle that ended close to three decades ago.

The MKMVA was meant to give those who had fought for MK access to political leadership and ensure that their integration into society happened smoothly. If this task has not been achieved in the twenty-seven years since the unbanning of MK, twenty-four years since MK dissolved and twenty-three years since the advent of ANC rule, then a question needs to be asked about the real reason for its existence. The MKMVA has gained more prominence during the Zuma presidency; wherever they are, there are clashes and scuffles with anti-Zuma protestors.

Maphatsoe himself is not a very bright chap, but he is loud, with a paucity of decorum – which makes him useful, I guess. An unfortunate incident in which his genitals were captured on a mobile phone camera – while he was reading the paper after what appears to be a liaison with a woman (who is not his wife) – went viral. He went quiet for a while; discussions about his tiny penis exploded on social media. Some time later, he must have decided that what he lacks in size, he would make up for in loudness.

He publicly accused Kasrils of having sent Fezekile to ensnare Zuma. Kasrils sued him for defamation, and was awarded R500 000 in damages – money that he pledged would be used for Fezekile's benefit.

Fezekile died two months later, but I know that Kasrils has had meetings with some who were close to Fezekile to discuss how the money could be used for Beauty's benefit.

Kasrils dismisses the honeytrap conspiracy. If such a plan existed, it was clearly the work of amateurs: Fezekile would have had the right people speaking to her immediately after being 'planted'; they would have made sure that samples from her, Zuma and the bed were taken early on, and that the passage of time did not allow for any erosion of evidence. Fezekile would not have been advised to wait a while before laying a charge – she would have done so immediately. The conspirators would have rehearsed her statement and ensured that, like Zuma's, it had professional input and was thus impervious to contradictions and inconsistencies. They would have ensured that she was protected from the media and that only the version that strengthened their case prevailed. Instead, a hapless Fezekile initially presented different versions of her story to different journalists. Hardly the actions of an adroit manipulator.

Even if there was a conspiracy, society needs to interrogate the easy pass that was given to Zuma and why a seasoned politician, senior leader and former intelligence head of a formidable liberation movement was exempt from agency and moral rectitude. Why was it so easy for him to fall for the 'trap'? Why was Zuma *allowed* to be the victim when, in Mmatshilo Motsei's words:[23]

> It was his hands that lowered the kanga and massaged [Fezekile] with baby oil; it had nothing to do with the invisible hand of a third force. It was his hands that turned her body around and his fingers that were inserted into her vagina; it had nothing to do with political camps. It was his arms that held her as he penetrated her; it had nothing to do with the arms deal.

In the first chapter of Motsei's book, she elegantly and succinctly captures the point that I have attempted to make several times: '[H]e was aware of the power he held over [Fezekile]; he knew that [...] he was a father-figure to her and had a moral obligation to exercise control over his sexual urges, especially if and when sex was initiated by her'. And, critically: 'Because of his strong belief in ancestors, Zuma must have known that the wrath of the spirit of his comrade who died in exile leaving behind a distraught ten-year-old daughter might come back to haunt him'.[24]

Kimmy has absolute disdain for peddlers of the honeytrap theory. If she had been a part of the honeytrap mob, why would Fezekile have messaged her to tell her something that she must already have known? It was to Kimmy that Fezekile had said 'he penetrated me', and Kimmy who had advised Fezekile to go to the doctor – a strange conversation between conspirators. Had Fezekile's message read 'It's done', or 'Mission accomplished', it would be clear that there was a common purpose and that Fezekile had fulfilled her requirements.

The anger in her voice – all these years later – when she talks about the idea is palpable:

> It was crazy and ridiculous. I could not believe it. I had nothing to gain from that. And, if anyone wanted to set up a honeytrap for [Zuma], sending Fez, one of his children, was a bad idea. How could anyone have known that sending his friend's child, whom he'd known since age five, could work? A decent person would be appalled at a sexual relationship between father and daughter. It was easy to assume that Zuma would be, too. If someone wanted to set him up, then the plan had a much better chance of succeeding if it involved a different woman.

· · ·

Under the trial's surface, the violence simmered. Fezekile was not the only one who feared for her safety. Her legal counsel was putting out fires of her own, under police guard. Adv de Beer confirms that, every afternoon while driving out of the court precinct, a mob would approach her car, banging hard on the vehicle as she drove off, shouting and hurling insults. Every day the shouting got louder and louder, the commentary more vicious.

She kept working.

I doubt that she was prepared for what lay ahead. I tried very hard to get her to confirm a few things that had happened to her personally, promising to steer clear of the legal arguments themselves, about which she is forbidden to speak.

'What do you want to know? I will let you know what I can and cannot answer.'

She did not expect my question. 'Is it true that you found snakes on your doorstep during the trial?'

The stunned look on her face is all the confirmation I need. She wants to know how I know something that was not in the public domain.

'Sources.'

In the many years for which she had been living on her property, she had never encountered a single snake. But one evening, a couple of snakes of the boomslang species were left on the doorstep at her home – at the height of the historic trial. She found the episode strange, but amusing. But her domestic worker, who was Zulu, and the black police officers who were assigned to guard her house, ran in all directions, screaming their lungs out. Her domestic worker refused to return until every sign of the snake had vanished. Even the police officers were visibly shaken. They believed it was a sign of witchcraft.

While Adv de Beer was fighting off snakes, Adv Broodryk was also witnessing strange happenings but he is reluctant, without proof, to link them to the trial. But he does share with me that, in all the years of being in court, he had never witnessed such animosity. 'That courtroom was full of seething anger and animosity. You could feel it land on your skin as you walked in and it lasted the entire trial.'

Broodryk and De Beer's race, culture and background are not assumed to hold any beliefs about, or gravitations towards, witchcraft, traditional medicine, spells, or whatever these events signified. Adv Broodryk says there was something sinister in the air and that, for the three days in which Adv de Beer cross-examined Zuma, she had been weak and ill. This was sudden and inexplicable, but she had soldiered on and made it through.

It gets even more bizarre. It is difficult to write about because I also personally have no extensive knowledge or experience of this world, save to say that I am aware that many believe and practise it. The trial took a heavy toll on Adv de Beer. Its aftermath was particularly brutal: her office was raided for no reason, her marriage fell apart and she took some heavy financial blows. Her health was so precarious that she had to stop exercising. She just could not figure out what was wrong with her. During her cross-examination of Zuma, she was so pale and weak that Adv Broodryk put his arm around her and asked her if she was okay; for the full three days, she was dizzy and experienced stomach cramps.

The trial had long ended and life had continued, so she did not make any association between her circumstances and the trial. But, ten years after the trial, a friend of hers went to consult a spiritual healer for personal reasons. She did not discuss this with Adv de Beer, as the matters for which she sought this healing were deeply personal. In fact, she had not spoken to Adv de Beer for some time, and they certainly had no reason to discuss the rape trial.

But, out of the blue, her friend called to inform her that the healer had told her that there was a spell over her that was linked to her interaction with Adv de Beer. She asked that Adv de Beer phone the healer, who traced the negative energy around her to a darkness that had been imposed on her many years before, during the rape trial.

A Zuma insider, at the nucleus of his political machinations, says a sangoma from rural KwaZulu-Natal had been brought to Johannesburg to fortify Zuma's home and be present in court during proceedings. According to this source, she was in court every day of the trial, despite not speaking a word of English.

The battle to save Zuma from a rape conviction and, by extension, to ensure his political survival was fought inside and outside the court-room, using every tactic imaginable. It does not matter whether any of these strategies worked, whether a sangoma could really weaken the opposition and determine the outcome of the trial.

What is important is that some believed it could.

The world moved on, but not everyone whom the trial's flames had burnt was able to move with it. Long after Judge van der Merwe made the closing statement of his judgment – 'In my judgment the state has not proved the accused's guilt beyond reasonable doubt. The accused is found not guilty and is discharged' – the smell of burnt-out embers lingered.

Legally, Zuma is not a rapist. As law expert Pierre de Vos says, 'PW Botha and FW De Klerk have never been found guilty of committing a crime. Does not mean they did nothing wrong. On the contrary.'[25] The trial and its aftermath presented the nation with a philosophical ques-tion: How are we to understand ourselves as a people, when we expect so little from those who lead?

Barney Mthombothi offers a sobering answer, an indictment of our society:[26]

It's not as if we didn't know. Khwezi, the woman who accused Zuma of rape, described the incident in graphic detail. She told of her horror on opening her eyes to see the man she's always regarded as a father stark naked and about to mount her. Picture the scene. Freezeframe it. Such a man we continue to call our president, a man worthy of respect.

Khwezi, meanwhile, has been hounded out of existence – nameless, faceless and even stateless. We still don't know her name; we still don't know what she looks like, or where she is or whether she's being looked after. We just don't care, because if we did Zuma wouldn't be our president.

As renowned former Constitutional Court judge Zak Yacoob said in 2014, 'I have a serious difference of opinion. I had a serious problem with the Zuma judgment', and also, 'There's an element of the subjective in a judge's decision-making process [...] I may have found differently because I would not have criticised the witness for not reporting the rape sooner, and for her sexual history.'[27] His next comment resonates with an important theme of this book – that there are many ways at arriving at and interpreting the truth and a court of law offers one way. It must be acknowledged that this is not a bad thing, otherwise many would be wrongly convicted based on the judge's own prejudice and philosophical leanings. The journey towards the truth is an arduous, fraught exercise. As Yacoob continues, 'Trials and judges do not decide the truth, judges never know the truth'; indeed, Yacoob 'believed the Zuma trial was not about finding the truth but a "story telling" contest between two opposing sides, with the judgment based on which side told the better story'.

I feel vindicated by this.

. . .

I asked Fezekile whether she had ever thought about what she would do if she lost the case.

'Not at the time that I laid the charge. I was just scared but defiant. No man was going to get away with this again.'

'And when you actually lost? What was your reaction, the first thing that came to your mind?'

She breathed heavily. Her mind seemed to be wandering. Not for the first time, I wondered whether I would get her back, if she would return to this moment. She had an irritating habit of doing this, wandering off and not coming back to finish a conversation we had started. It happened when she was overwhelmed or stressed by a topic. Sometimes, she couldn't seem to keep quiet and would go on until she had run out of words. But sometimes, she just switched off.

Hours later, when I had long given up on a response, she sent me an SMS stating that losing was not the end of the matter for her. 'I did not do it to win. There was no contest. I was just fighting for myself.'

'But did that fight seem more bruising because the case was lost? Would it not be comforting to have received justice?'

'It depends what you mean by justice.'

'How do you understand the concept of justice, in relation to the case?'

'If by justice you mean the rapist going to jail, then that is not how I see it. It is not how I believe it. But if by justice you mean not being victimised, called names, doubted, not having Ma sick from it all, not being followed, not being poor as a result of this sordid affair, then maybe we are talking.'

'So, there was no justice as far as you are concerned because in the second part of your message, you have just described your life in the last ten years and possibly your life as a child.'

'Bingo. Paradise, nè?'

CHAPTER 6

Zuma in the dock

In the face of such intense legal scrutiny of Fezekile's life, we need, perhaps, to remind ourselves that Jacob Zuma was the one on trial. A look
at Adv de Beer's cross-examination of Zuma, and how it contrasted
with Adv Kemp's line of questioning, reveals a great deal about the
accused.

Zuma's defence did a sterling job of downplaying the father–daughter, or uncle–niece, relationship that Fezekile claimed to have with
Zuma. The two of them had not seen each other for about fourteen
years. Adv Kemp argued that this, coupled with the fact that Fezekile
had not called Zuma and told him about her HIV status during that
time, meant that they could not have been close and she had no reason
to consider Zuma a father.

The difficulty here is that, in court, a brilliant Afrikaans advocate
appeared in front of the Afrikaans Judge van der Merwe to argue
against a cultural aspect and way of life that were unfamiliar to both
men. In 2004, seventeen years after I had lost my own father, I went
about researching the circumstances of his death. I had not seen many of
his friends since the late 1980s, but I remembered them and where they
had lived. I rounded them up, visiting them in their homes, interviewing

them for hours on end. They received me as their daughter, with some of them saying they wished my father had lived to see how his little girl had turned out. I was an adult, but still my father's little girl. They knew this.

The passage of time does not alter these bonds. A parent figure, associate, friend, or contemporary of your parent remains your parent for all time. Zuma knew this very well.

Judson's comrades all confirmed that the bonds that were formed with one another's families and children were unique, and that exile was an environment in which everyone knew everyone and children were, in some instances, raised communally. The children belonged to all the uncles and aunties. In other words, a comrade's child was a no-go area.

To Adv Kemp's question, 'In which way is he [Zuma] your father if he has not really seen you at that time for 14 years since 1985?' Fezekile's response was an eloquent and clear reflection of the complex layers of human relationships:

> Perhaps it is important for me at this point to explain a few things. My first memories of my life are in exile. As a child in exile all the elderly men that were there were Malumes and the women were Aunties. It was a kind of communal parenting if you want, for lack of a better word [...] basically everybody was everybody's parent and everybody's child.

She then explains why, even after returning to South Africa, years after she had last seen him, Zuma remained particularly special to her:

> And for me firstly Malume Zuma behaved as the same person that I had remembered him as a child to be, and secondly because of

his particular closeness to my father, from my own memory firstly, secondly from my mother's tales and other comrades' tales and also from his own tale that he told me I felt close to him as a father more than other Malumes.

Even when questioning Kimmy, Kemp doggedly tried to convince the court that Zuma and Fezekile could not have had a father–daughter, uncle–niece relationship. He even wanted to know the year in which Fezekile started regarding Zuma as a father figure: 'So you have no idea when this regarding him as her father started?'

'Exact date sir, no,' Kimmy replied.

'The year?'

'I believe it is more than a year.'

'More than a year?'

'Yes.'

'And what did she say to you? I now regard Malume as my father?'

'No she did not say I now regard Malume as my father [...] and she had before actually also made reference to him in terms of talking about her father and she was saying it is actually quite nice to have Malume there because he is that connection with my father.'

I first encountered 'Uncle' and 'Auntie' So-and-So when I went to a multiracial school and heard white kids refer to their friends' mothers and fathers in that way. Prior to that, in the township, adults and our parents' friends were 'Papa' and 'Mama' So-and-So. For black children who came from black families and black communities but who went to school with white children and encountered different cultures, 'father' and 'uncle' may have had the same meaning. But, in court, Kimmy and Fezekile had to defend their regard for Zuma as a father figure painstakingly, and were questioned about their assumptions that he knew they regarded him as such.

'But then how do you know that he regarded, he knew that she [Fezekile] regarded him as a father?' Kemp asked Kimmy.

Zuma knew. By virtue of his relationship with Judson and Beauty, Fezekile's age and his Zulu culture, he knew. At this point, it becomes irrelevant how she regarded him. What is relevant is what *he* understood by their relationship, based on his cultural beliefs. He, the traditionalist, *must* have known that she was his daughter.

Later, he asks Kimmy if Zuma 'spoke to [Kimmy] as a peer or as a child'.

The question itself, using Zuma's belief in culture and tradition, is outrageous. He should be appalled at the thought of Kimmy being anything other than a child to him.

She answers, 'As a child.'

'So did he know that you regarded him as a father figure as well?'

'I would hope so.'

These relationships and roles are never discussed. You could say they are predetermined, ordained by fate. The rules of the cultural beliefs that Zuma claims to hold dear dictate that your friends' children are your children. Whether a white Afrikaans advocate knew this, I do not know. But I believe he did, because Afrikaans culture observes the same deference for authority and adults.

Consider Fezekile, thirty-one years old in 2005, and Zuma, sixty-three. More than twice her age. A friend of her late father. A friendship that his lawyers tried to minimise during the trial, but one to which several people attest. Many know that Jacob and Judson were brothers, comrades and friends. Judson did not live to see the fruits of democracy, the South Africa for which he had fought become a reality. He could not have imagined that the new South Africa would bring untold pain to his family.

People who supported Fezekile talk of the 'damage'. Kimmy remembers, all too well, the threatening calls from comrades, aunts and uncles of the struggle. 'The aunties were particularly vicious and angry. They told us to back off, that we were ruining Zuma's life, we were ruining the movement. It was horrific.'

Kimmy's version is confirmed by so many of Fezekile's supporters and friends, some of whom allege that their homes were under surveillance during that time.

'Those days were horrible, Redi. The phone calls did not stop. We lost a whole lot of people. People who had been in our lives forever. People to whom we looked up. We lost them. Their accusations stung. It was ridiculous. What they were prepared to do for Zuma.'

'I notice you keep calling him Zuma. What happened to "uncle"?'

'I stopped calling him "uncle" the day Fez told me he'd raped her. I do not recognise him. He is Zuma.'

This is quite a transition. Kimmy disputes the argument that, because Fezekile and Zuma had not seen each other in years, they were not close: 'I also had not seen Zuma in a while but he was an uncle. We did not keep in touch daily but he was our uncle. Fezeka regarded him as a father.' At the trial, Kimmy had said, 'He is the person that she could go to with her trouble, you know, an adult figure or a father figure you know, in that sense.'

Kimmy tells me that, on the day Thabo Mbeki fired Zuma as deputy president, she saw him from a distance just outside Parliament. 'I tried to run to him, just to give him a hug, but he was surrounded by his security and in no time, he was gone.'

Later that week, Kimmy had called Fezekile and suggested they organise a lunch at Zuma's home. It would be a small family affair, to comfort him and cheer him up.

'I called Zuma and proposed the idea. He was very pleased that his children wanted to do this for him.'

'And by children, you mean ...'

'Not just his biological children. Us, the children who regarded him as a father figure. I called a few people to organise this. Fez was there, as one of his children, in his house.'

Fezekile made a big deal of these relationships with her father's comrades. She treasured them and enjoyed hearing stories about Judson, gravitating towards anyone who could keep his memory alive. It was distressing to her and to Kimmy that accepted norms were rubbished in court and they were supposed to provide a date on which they had started regarding their struggle uncles as father figures. In the judge's and advocate's world, 'father figure' meant something different, perhaps – regular contact in a formalised relationship. But in African traditions there is no formalising such relationships. Even adoption is not governed by paperwork and officialdom. Children of blood relatives who lose their parents or who, for some reason, cannot be taken care of by their parents can be 'adopted' without going through the bureaucratic process. By virtue of their being younger than the adults around them, they are regarded as children of the family; by virtue of the adults' being old enough to be their parents, they are truly regarded as mothers and fathers. So, Zuma's version, as presented to the court and to Kimmy during her cross-examination, is a distortion of the cultural norms that govern relationships in African society.

'Can I put to you the accused's version of this is, he says there was a bond of loyalty between the comrades and their families forged by the peculiar shared history, and if there were any comrades of families or their children that he could help he would help them, but that does not make each and every one of them his family,' Kemp put to Kimmy.

'It is correct he did help kids or comrades where he could, but my comment is that he knew that Fezeka regarded him as a father figure.'

'How did he know? What did he say to you?'

'Sir, you do not just call someone Malume and have that much respect for them if you do not regard them in that particular light [...].'

Kimmy went on to emphasise that the way people communicate – the way they address one another and the topics they discuss – informs their regard for one another. She argued that there is a major difference between how a person would relate to and address 'a peer' and an adult whom they regard as a father figure or an uncle. And that, from her observations, Fezekile addressed Zuma as one would a father figure, and Zuma himself acted in kind. But in court she was required to prove that Zuma knew that Fezekile regarded him as a father. She was expected to provide the clinical facts for when this father–daughter relationship began. This is not something that could be proven, governed, as it was, by unwritten societal mores and the undocumented practices that defined communities.

The court made no provision for the complexities of human relations and the conventions by which these relations are adjudicated – it was a case of what could and could not be proven. But Zuma sat there, knowing what Kimmy meant – that, in the same way she could easily argue with a peer, she could not do so with him. That if she were to call a peer 'hey *wena*', she could not address Zuma in that manner; if she could swear in front of a peer, she could not do so in front of Zuma; if she could say to a peer, 'Go and make your own tea,' she could not reject Zuma's request for such.

This is how these relationships play out in our homes and communities – and what confirmed to Kimmy and Fezekile that Zuma must have known the rules, but chose to exploit them.

In her cross-examination of Zuma, Adv de Beer touches on these rules. Reading this part of the transcript, I know that Zuma and his supporters knew that Adv de Beer was adroit in asking the next question, 'She did not call you on your name: hallo Jacob. She called you Malume?'

'Yes M'Lord that is true because according to Zulu tradition a child will never call you by the name.'

They go around in circles, with Zuma testifying that if Fezekile used 'hlonipha language' (respectful language), she would have called him uBaba (Father).

Adv de Beer then states, 'She in fact testified that very occasionally she did call you uBaba.'

Zuma: 'That is possible. I would not dispute it.'

In her cross-examination, Adv de Beer also navigates power and responsibility.

'What was your attitude to possible sex or relations between you, were you disinterested, interested, against it, for it?' she asks. This is where Zuma's worldview, his lack of discernment, and his failure to appreciate the depth of his moral depravity are most evident. In truth, Adv de Beer's question was the perfect escape for someone who believed he had been lured into having sex or had given in after much reluctance or resistance. It offered Zuma an opportunity to claim that, until that moment, he had never contemplated 'having sex' with Khwezi – that everything had happened so quickly, hence his deep regrets. But vintage Zuma, flippant and defiant, answers, 'I had no problem with having sexual intercourse with her bearing in mind that she had (indistinct) and I did not have any problem if we had to go to bed and have sexual intercourse.'

Adv de Beer's cross-examination also gives fascinating insights into his inability to reflect on the moral responsibility that comes with being an elder. When asked why he went ahead with 'intercourse' with an HIV-positive woman without a condom, he answers, 'Both of us wanted to have sexual intercourse, our needs dictated to us.' He answers the question, of course, but not in a way that traces responsibility back to himself. He is not being asked why Fezekile 'went ahead'. He is being asked why *he* went ahead, and masterfully removes the spotlight from his own behaviour by invoking the collective '*we*'.

In addition, Michael Hulley, Zuma's lawyer, initially denied that anything had happened between Zuma and Fezekile in an interview with CapeTalk's Mike Wills on 14 November 2006. This interview was used as an exhibit in the trial. It was only after DNA test results proved otherwise that Zuma conceded that 'consensual' sex had occurred.

Also worth noting is that Zuma knew himself to be HIV-negative, but had not had an HIV test for seven years at the time of the incident. In those seven years, he had had relationships, marriages and children with multiple partners. So, he could not have been certain of his status on 2 November. Yet it was Fezekile's status that was presented negatively, as if she was a woman who slept around so much that she did not even know who had infected her and when that may have happened.

Adv de Beer presses Zuma on this point, that he could not have known his status and could not argue that he was negative on the night in question.

'How did you know that for sure?'

'I had tested and secondly I had a way of having intercourse with the people that I had intercourse with.'

There is that male power, that privilege to which many who have it are so blind. A man can – in broad daylight, with his wives, children and other lovers watching and listening – in a court, filled with members of the public and the gaze of the international media, tell the world about the multiple people with whom he has had sex. He was assured that nobody would gasp, nobody would call him names. Yes, we knew he was a polygamist, but here he was demonstrating that he was a philanderer as well – a man who had sex with other 'people'. He would not be censured or judged, however, because male privilege and power, and society's complicity, had spun a protective cocoon around him.

Zuma then admits that he has preached the safe sex message many times, which is the policy of the government he once represented and the party that had elected him as its deputy president – a position he still held during the trial. As the deputy president of the country, he headed the Moral Regeneration Movement, which promoted – preached – condom use. Yet, when asked whether his conduct that night had not dealt a huge blow to the government's message, he answered, '[…] whilst I knew what the stance of the Government was I did not by so doing think that I was actually giving a blow to the Government by so doing.'

Zuma continues, 'Though [Fezekile] ordinarily would not agree to have unprotected sex but on this night in question she insisted after she had noticed that I was hesitant, she said you cannot just leave it at this.' Zuma, soon to be president of the country and ANC, a former MK commander and prominent leader of the anti-apartheid struggle would have us believe that he was hesitant, but had been pushed by a woman half his age, the daughter of his comrade, to have sex. That he had been powerless.

The court heard that Fezekile had not had sex without a condom since 1996. The encounter with Zuma would have been her first exposure to unprotected sex. But Zuma regularly had unprotected sex with his wives – and, we presume, lovers, because some of the women with whom he had children were not married to him at that time. De Beer uses this to argue that 'the fact that you had intercourse that night without a condom was an indication that she was actually raped because she would never have consented to sex with you without a condom?'

'That is not true, she had consented, she actually took the initiative, when she noticed that I was being hesitant she encouraged me.'

As a woman, Adv de Beer could not have been blind to the significance of Zuma's power, which is likely why she introduced the theme of power and responsibility. It is difficult to read, in Zuma's answer, whether he has the same appreciation for his formidable power, or chooses to be obtuse and play the fool. Adv de Beer questions him about his various leadership positions – the deputy presidency that he held for six years before being fired by Mbeki, and the deputy presidency of the ANC: 'And then your position as the Deputy President of the ANC which you have still got is also a very important and powerful position, not so?'

'Yes.'

On his role as leader of the Moral Regeneration Movement, she asks, 'And that movement was all about bringing back the morals, the values, the customs, the traditions and so forth, not so?'

'Yes.'

'In fact you said in an interview with the *Mail & Guardian* on 6 May that "we want to create a society where the value that underpinned my upbringing, that everybody's child is my child, is regenerated".'

With no sense of irony, Zuma answers, 'Yes.'

Later, Adv de Beer asks, 'You were indeed best friends with the complainant's deceased father [Judson] Kuzwayo?'

'Yes that is true.' Zuma admits, with ease, that not only were they friends, they were best friends.

Under pressure from Adv de Beer, he concedes that it is not just Judson he would visit in Swaziland, Lesotho and Zambia, but Judson's family as well – and that he would play with the children.

'So your relationship with the Kuzwayos can indeed be described as a family friend?'

'No. No I would say it was a comradely friendship.'

'Did it ever turn into a family friend relationship?'

'Never.'

Zuma was prepared to downplay his deep connection with Judson and his family, prepared to reduce what he had earlier conceded to be a close relationship ('best friends') to something superficial, just to save his own skin. His testimony in court contradicts the statement he made to the police, referred to as Exhibit L in the court record: 'I became acquainted to [Fezekile] through her families, both parents with comrades in the ANC. I continued to remain, our friendship after the death of her father.' Connections with late friends' families often end when those friends die – not immediately, granted, but over time as the pressures of life take over. But so deep and close was this friendship that it continued for years after Judson had died. Yet Zuma does not think it was special, that it should have ruled Fezekile out as a lover.

When challenged in court yet again, Zuma blames this on his attorney, Michael Hulley: 'As regards the other exhibit, this was what was said by my attorney maybe according to his observations. I did not say that.' Hulley could not have 'observed' that Zuma and the Kuzwayos were family friends; wasn't there, in exile. When Adv de Beer asks, 'Where did [Hulley] get it from?', Zuma answers, 'Well I would not know. Like I said maybe that is how he observed or how he learned.'

It is also important to explore what Zuma and Fezekile usually spoke about when they met. Remember, Zuma had observed that she wanted him and was determined to have him. He used her presence in his home, her kanga and her 'request' for a massage as proof. Yet the conversations prior to that were always about family, her work, her HIV status and, most dominantly, Judson. Zuma knew that Fezekile wanted to make contact with all the people who had shared a life with her father, because she wanted to write a book about him.

Adv de Beer asked, 'But because of all the stories and your closeness with her father, she really wanted to hear all about him from you because he died so early in her life?'

'That did not apply to me only. She told me that she would like to contact all the people who used to be with her father, close to her father, because she wanted to write a book about all that.'

'But what I am really getting at is that she was talking a lot to you about her father?'

'Well when we have met she would talk to me about her father, yes.'

Zuma even remembers Fezekile's favourite story about Judson. When asked about it, he answered, 'Well that applies to all the children, but as regards food I was actually referring to the stage when his father and I had only a loaf to share and she had interest in that particular story.'

I asked Fezekile why this particular story was so important to her. Without a pause, she launched into a deeply reflective narrative: 'I am not a Christian. But sharing bread has a religious and soulful meaning. Jesus shared bread with his "men" at the last supper. He only did that with people he loved and trusted. And it was the last supper, death came and they were parted. But first, they had shared something so simple, so beautiful. That is how I saw this sharing of bread between my father and him.'

She went on to add, 'And can you imagine, these two big men, no possessions in the world. Nothing but their love for their country. And having nothing to eat, except bread, but they were fighting on and sharing the little that they had. I thought it was special. Don't you?'

Of all the questions posed to Zuma during cross-examination, this one is the most significant and tells me, at least, that Zuma is oblivious to ethical conduct – blind, when it suits him, to his power and how it bends others to his will. Or, perhaps not blind, but he certainly refuses to assume the responsibilities that this power confers on him.

'Can you dispute the fact that she took you as a father figure?'

'I would not dispute it if she regarded me as that, but she knew for a fact that I am her father's friend. We are comrades who are close to one another.'

Fezekile knew, he says? If *she*, then, is the one behaving inappropriately, does he not take responsibility, reprimand her, and tell her that he regards her as a friend's child, treats her like he treats the other children (which he argued several times in his testimony), and cannot countenance a sexual encounter with her?

Power being the hallmark of this incident, Adv de Beer asks, 'It is clear if we go back to what we just said, that you are an authoritative and a powerful person, and that you had all these public positions, that she is not on the same level as you at all?'

'Yes,' he answers.

She then goes to the heart of the matter – the prism that has occupied so many of us, the single issue that has been collapsed in the interests of the law's narrow pursuit of what happened and how it happened, the one factor that demonstrates the limitations of the law. Power, and how it is experienced by those who do not have it.

She asks, 'There is in fact this absolute and massive power imbalance between the two of you?'

His answer tells us everything we need to know about him: 'Well I do not know what that is supposed to mean, because we do not work in the same place.'

Even Fezekile's dress code was subjected to Zuma's worldview, as Adv de Beer's cross-examination shows.

'M'Lord,' Zuma says, 'like I said earlier on that she used to come to my place dressed in pants, but on this occasion she came dressed in a skirt. And the way she was sitting in that lounge was not the usual way that I know her to be sitting. That was not usual of her […].'

They then debate the length of the skirt, with Zuma answering that it came 'up to the knee level'.

Adv de Beer: 'And then you said something about the way she was sitting in the lounge.'

'Yes.'

'What was peculiar about that?'

'M'Lord what I mean by that is that under normal circumstances if a woman is dressed in a skirt she would sit properly with her legs together, but she was sitting anyhow, she did not cross her legs, she would not even wonder or mind if the [skirt] was raised or came up.'

From this, Zuma decided 'that well there is something that she is after ...'

It is important to mention that Zuma had also told the court, earlier, that Fezekile was emotional and unsettled when she came to his home. She was very anxious about her niece's child, the snakebite victim. So distraught was she that she was willing to travel to Swaziland, late at night, to be with the child. But in court, in Zuma's mind, she could switch from that level of distress to seduction and sex.

Later in the cross-examination, we get another insight into Zuma. His commentary may have made headlines because of its outrageousness, but we are yet to subject it to a thorough analysis as a reflection on the abuse of power and what he was and is willing to do to escape accountability. It appears there is always someone to blame, or some cultural belief – known only to Zuma – to explain his bizarre positions. Regarding Zuma's view of Fezekile's 'arousal', Adv de Beer asks, 'Yes and you have explained that the way you grew up or in the Zulu culture you do not leave a woman in that situation. She will have you arrested and say you are a rapist?'

'Yes,' Zuma replied, 'I was trying to explain that as I was growing up as a young boy in my tradition I was told if you get to that stage with a woman and you do not do anything further whilst she is at that stage, it is said she becomes so infuriated that she can even lay a false charge against you and allege that you have raped her.'

This tradition is known only to Zuma. Only he knows by whom 'it is said' that women become 'so infuriated' that they would go as far as facing the humiliation and stigmatisation that comes with rape.

Zuma kept returning to the same point – that he understood Fezekile was upset that he had not called her after they'd had intercourse, which is what his emissaries had told him. It implied that she would accuse him of rape simply because he hadn't called – because she felt used and neglected. I never got to speak to Fezekile about this, but Kimmy reacted quite emotionally when I asked her: 'I mean, how stupid do they think Fez was? She was a grown woman in her early 30s, she'd been in relationships that hadn't worked out before.'

To me, though, this reveals something else – Zuma's entitlement and ego. Even according to his version – that the sex was consensual – he is still exercising noxious power and demonstrating insatiable greed and disregard for her dignity. After their 'consensual' encounter, he had no regard for her well-being, no desire to check whether she had reached work safely the next day, and made no attempt to have one of his drivers take her home. This is the normal interaction of people who have just been intimate with – and, according to Zuma, enjoyed – each other: a call, perhaps, or a flirtatious message about the night. He was ready to take what he claims was offered, but nothing stopped him from affording her courtesy and respect afterwards. He simply ejaculated in her, got out of bed to shower, and forgot her.

'Yes I remember that when I was asked because I said she was upset maybe because I did not contact her to ask her how she fared in her journey,' Zuma said under cross-examination.

Later, Adv de Beer asks, 'So was there a duty upon you to phone her to ask her about her journey to work?'

'No that was not my responsibility.' Cold and entitled. No regard for a woman who, according to him, was his lover. Here, he lived up to his name: Gedleyihlekisa, one who destroys you while laughing at you.

Zuma may have been acquitted, but Fezekile stood by her version, a version that was presented more emphatically in the last few minutes of Adv de Beer's cross-examination:

'I put it to you that you went back to the guest room that night to rape her when she was fast asleep,' she stated.

'That is not true,' Zuma replied.

'That you approached her already naked from the curtain side.'

'That is true.'

'And started to wake her up in a manner that would have raised no alarm bell.'

'That is not true.'

'You raped her regardless of her three "No Malumes" and the clear body language that she is not consenting.'

'No, that is not so.'

'She froze when she saw your naked body on top of her.'

'No, that is not true.'

'You penetrated her without a condom and without her consent.'

'It was consensual sex although I did not have a condom.'

'The penetration caused her extreme discomfort because of the friction.'

'No, that is not true.'

'You held her hands throughout the rape.'

'No, that is not true.'

'And you spoke to her during the rape in an attempt to get her attention as her behaviour and body language bothered and worried you.'

'That is not so.'

This is the version that Fezekile took to her grave.

• • • • • • • •

CHAPTER 7

Back into exile

The day after the trial concluded, Fezekile and her mother left South Africa for their second exile. Their country, their home, had spat them out.

Fezekile told me that, whether she had won the case or not, she reckoned they would still have had to live their lives on the run. Simply put, they had been hounded out.

During the trial, their house in KwaMashu, a township in KwaZulu-Natal, was burned down. It is suspected that Zuma supporters were the perpetrators, but no one was arrested for this crime. There is no doubt that this criminal act was meant to scare Fezekile and Beauty into submission.

Added to this, her public near-lynching during every day of the trial made living in South Africa untenable. It would be unfair to say, without proof, that Zuma was behind all of this. But the fact remains that he did not call off his bloodthirsty supporters. At no point did he demonstrate the rectitude of a leader and instruct them to respect legal processes. While Fezekile was being threatened with death right outside the court, not once did Zuma use the many platforms available to him and say, *Not in my name*. Even if he had been falsely accused, he had a responsibility to ensure that his supporters respected the laws of the country he was so hungry to lead.

Like most townships, KwaMashu is an eclectic mix of classes and lifestyles, but is mainly poor and working-class. It cannot be said that comrades joined the struggle to become rich, but it is a fact, nonetheless, that very few families of high-ranking ANC officials and former MK commanders live the way Fezekile and Beauty lived. Democracy has been kind to many ANC leaders. Those who are not rich are comfortable: they live a suburban life with access to good schools and quality jobs. Former ANC and MK leaders went on to take up senior positions in the new civil service; those who kept their old township homes did so by choice.

That Fezekile and Beauty had remained stuck in the township despite Judson's seniority was telling. Their tiny home was neglected, unfenced. It could have done with some upkeep – basic things like tiles, cupboards, paint, an extension for a bathroom. Fezekile spoke of times when they did not even have money to eat. They had received a once-off pension that the new government gave to former MK soldiers and families of those who had lost their lives in the fight against apartheid. It was hardly a lot of money. With their need for housing, food and Fezekile's education, the money soon ran out. Her rent, medication and special diet, and her mom's medication, meant that life constantly seemed to demand far more than she could provide, emotionally and materially.

Stan Thula, a medical specialist from KwaMashu, has known the family for years. His childhood home is a few houses from Beauty's. He told me that, whereas they were not destitute, they deserved more dignity – even before the trial: 'Returning from exile without her husband, with a young woman to educate, must have been tough for MaBeauty.'

Beauty would have been approaching fifty when the ANC was unbanned and exiled families were returning. It would have been difficult for anyone to reinvent himself or herself and start again after returning to a country he or she had left many years ago.

'That fire was harder on Ma than on me. I was busy having an out-of-body experience. Do you know what that is like?' Fezekile told me.

'No, I can't say I do.'

She went on to describe a shutting down of sorts, where she willed her mind not to register anything, her eyes not to see and her ears not to hear. But, most importantly, she worked on her heart 'every day', begging it not to feel anything.

'Did you succeed?'

'No, I did not, dear. The heart has a mind of its own. I felt. I felt a lot of things.'

'Like?'

'Fear and loathing.' And, 'You see, dear, when it became clear that my life was in danger, from the threats that people were making, I was consumed by that, the fear for Ma and I not knowing what the future holds, what might become of us. That kinda took me by surprise, the hatred, it was thick, all over, even in the air I breathed, you know.'

Zuma's star was rising in the trial's aftermath. His victory had been a euphoric moment. He had received Judge van der Merwe's ruling stoically, but multiple sources who were close to him at that time say he had been genuinely frightened and anxious. He had sat still and seemed impenetrable in court as the judge had delivered the historic judgment. Vintage Zuma, he had saved his emotions and performance for the masses gathered outside. A master of the politics of spectacle, he knew where his power lay and understood the language of the streets. Some supporters had been bused in; others had gone religiously to the court precinct every day to cheer him on. It was to these adoring crowds that Zuma had accounted. His advisers, comrades and daughter beside him, he had rendered his famous '*Mshini Wami*' – 'Bring me my machine gun' – a struggle song about the machine gun sung by MK soldiers during the fight against apartheid. No doubt it had been a message to his enemies, people who he believed were fighting him, trying to prevent him from becoming president.

At a deeper – allegorical – level, however, the machine gun represented obscene power, violence and control: all the characteristics of the crime of which he had been accused. The machine gun was a phallic symbol. In fact, modern parlance colloquially refers to the penis as *mshini wami*. It was a most inappropriate song, under the circumstances, but power seldom holds a mirror to its own face. It does what power does: determinedly pursues its target, using other people's lives as stepping stones.

The trial was a major hurdle for him to have overcome. His victory reverberated throughout the country as he rode the wave.

The day after his acquittal, on 9 May 2006, Zuma arrived at the radio station for which I worked, Talk Radio 702, to address the nation and issue his apology.[28] In his statement, he asked for Fezekile's rights to be respected. But it was too late. She and her mother had already had to turn their backs on a hostile country.

What happened behind the scenes as his apology was being formulated reflects deeply on Zuma's psychology. According to sources who were part of Zuma's fight-back strategy, Zuma had not seen, initially, a need to apologise. In his view, he had been acquitted, and the matter ended there. Zwelinzima Vavi, Blade Nzimande, Lakela Kaunda and Zweli Mkhize had persuaded him to apologise. Vavi tells me, 'Absolutely, I insisted that he apologise.' And Nzimande confirms that he advised Zuma to apologise.

The apology he issued had been crafted by his aides and worked on by several people. Also present at the time were Michael Hulley, Ranjeni Munusamy, Nzimande and Vavi. He had sat quietly and sometimes dozed off, or let his mind wander, as it often did during important deliberations. He had given no input when the apology and statement were discussed. The message had not come from deep within his heart, from profound reflection and contrition. Several members of his advisory team told me that 'he did not come up with this apology himself. It was what he was told to do. He was told he had to do it'.

I ask them whether, at any point, Zuma had expressed regret privately about what had happened, about the situation he had created with Fezekile – any sign that he wished he could turn back the clock.

'No, no, he just does not see what he did wrong.'

'Even if he says it was consensual, was there not even a concession, expressed privately to you guys, that he should not have even thought of his comrade's daughter in that way?'

'Nope. In his mind, they were out to get him.'

'Did he say anything about Judson Kuzwayo?'

'Nope.'

Fezekile's friend and colleague Shaun Mellors was instrumental in securing her and Beauty's passage to the Netherlands. Shaun, the director of the International HIV/AIDS Alliance, and Fezekile met at the XIII International Aids Conference in Durban in July 2000. It was a historic conference at the height of Thabo Mbeki's Aids denialism. (The powerful appeal to Mbeki's heart by Nkosi Johnson, a child living with Aids, is a poignant chapter in South Africa's history. Johnson, an emaciated eight-year-old boy, stood on the global stage, begging the president of his country to make affordable, life-saving antiretroviral treatment available to all. Mbeki had sat there, unmoved. Eventually, the courts and unrelenting civil society activism forced the government's hand. But it would be too late for Johnson, who died the following year.)

When Ronnie Kasrils first spoke to Fezekile and Beauty about my wish to write about and meet them, Shaun was the first person whom Fezekile phoned about my request. I had never met Shaun. As a South African who lived in London, he was familiar with my work. Fezekile told me I had 'passed the Shaun test'.

It is ironic, really, that Fezekile was part of the ARV movement and began an enduring friendship with Shaun, who, until today, is an advocate of ARVs – yet she made a different choice for herself. She went off ARVs and would not be persuaded to resume them, even when her health was deteriorating.

Fezekile worked initially in the alliance's cultural programme, then moved to the skills support programme and, eventually, to a programme that aimed to strengthen local communities and their response to Aids after the global conference. Shaun says Fezekile also officiated at his commitment ceremony to his then husband, in 2003. But in the UK, Shaun tells me, 'She missed Ma too much and she was placed in a role that focused on people living with HIV. It was a big role and there was a lot of pressure on her and so she decided to come back.'

Shaun, like many others, confirms that Fezekile had always been into alternative medicine, precisely because she believed it would keep her alive, not kill her. That is why he is also among those who do not believe that she chose death over life – that death is not something she invited or willingly walked towards. She rejected ARVs, he believes, not because she wanted to die, but because she believed there were healthier alternatives.

Before the trial, Shaun recalls, Fezekile led a reasonably healthy and busy life, working in the NGO sector. They stayed in touch and formed a solid friendship. Shaun was surprised when Fezekile did not turn up at his fortieth birthday one Saturday evening. The next day, he was shocked when he read the Sunday paper headlines, with one paper reporting the rape charge and another denying it.

'It was incredible. I could not believe it. It was complete shock and horror.'

While Fezekile was in the safe house during the trial, she stayed in touch with Shaun and a few friends, telling them how scared she was. In the early days of the trial, Shaun had got up in court and put some beads around Fezekile's neck. She wore the beads every day. Looking at Shaun now, a few months after her passing, I see that he wears the same beads. Fezekile saw the beads as a source of comfort and protection. When they broke, she frantically called Shaun – who was in London by then, thousands of kilometres away – and asked, 'What does it mean if the beads break?'

Shaun calmly said, 'Well, it means that the beads broke, nothing more, nothing less!'

Shaun tells me that he believes many people let Fezekile down. We spend some time discussing Fezekile's diary, the Zuma defence's trump card – and how nobody knows who handed the diary over to them, but everybody knows that it was used effectively and cruelly. When she expressed her shock at its being presented in court, the defence advocate admonished her, telling her it was irrelevant how he had acquired it.

Shaun tells me how he used his contacts in Amsterdam and activists from the One in Nine Campaign to help Fezekile and Beauty leave the country.

They left everything behind, boarding a KLM flight to start a new life.

'How did they apply for visas while still at the safe house? I mean, the trial ended and they were gone. How did that happen?' I ask.

Shaun laughs and his eyes come alive.

'Redi, it was nothing short of a miracle. I phoned a few friends, asking them to donate money to buy the tickets and to create a home for them in Amsterdam. I approached the embassy in Pretoria.'

Shaun had visited Fezekile and Beauty at safe houses in Johannesburg and Pretoria. 'It was like a scene from a movie,' he says. 'I had to meet these security people at McDonald's. I did not know who they were but they would put me in a car and drive me to a safe house to see Fez and Ma and then bring me back to McDonald's.'

In the meantime, Fezekile and Shaun had broken the rules by communicating constantly via SMS.

'I applied for their Dutch visas but I had to get photographs of them in order to apply. I asked her, "Fez, how are we going to do this?" She said, "Ma and I often go to movies so you can just happen to appear at the movie house and pretend you are just bumping into us and then I can give you the two photographs."'

The plan worked. With security guards escorting them, Fezekile and Beauty went to movies and 'bumped' into Shaun – who just happened to be there and reacted with a sunny 'Hi Fezeka! Fancy seeing you here.'

While they were hugging, Fezekile slipped their passport photos into Shaun's top pocket.

'I went to the embassy and applied for their visas. And I told the embassy that these are visas for Jacob Zuma's rape accuser. They want to get out of the country, there is absolutely nothing that they can do.'

Shaun is full of praise for the Dutch. They did not ask too many questions and were flexible, adjusting the rules to suit the situation and understanding that the applicants had restricted movement and could not present themselves personally. It also helped that he had a great contact within the embassy who worked on HIV programmes.

'And I think they also clearly saw what was happening in the court case.'

I imagine Shaun is referring to the threats, the vitriol and the sheer hatred. 'Once the pair arrived in Amsterdam,' he continues, 'they were issued with permits and everything they needed to access grants, and were given an apartment. It was really impressive.'

Fezekile told me in a conversation that 'life could have been worse. I am grateful to Amsterdam. They took us in and we lived. It was not a perfect life, but we lived.'

'Fez got on with life initially,' Shaun recalls. 'It was hard in some respects but she was positive, had so many plans and wanted a new life.'

Fezeka and Beauty stayed in Amsterdam from May 2006 until early 2010. They had a lot of support and soon made friends. Returning home was not an option. They had no idea what tomorrow would bring. Beauty became active in a local church and took up sewing to keep herself busy.

When Fezekile and Beauty arrived in Amsterdam, Raoul Fransen met them at the airport. Shaun had arranged for him to be there. Raoul introduced them to his close friends Peter van Rooijen and Jacqueline Wittebrood. Jacqueline remembers meeting Fezekile on a summer's day – she recalls Fezekile's 'fierce eyes', and says Beauty looked fragile but 'oh, so kind'. These were among the first people Fezekile and Beauty met in the immediate aftermath of the trial, when their fear was still palpable.

'To be frank,' Jacqueline tells me, 'I was a bit scared for them as I thought someone might come after them. It took me a little while to understand it was not necessarily the South African government she was fleeing from, but rather the mobs in the street who were after her.'

Their first home was a small studio in the Jordaan, a famous part of the Amsterdam city centre where workers used to live in the old days. Jacqueline has a vivid recollection of their home on the ground floor: 'The door looked like a barn or garage door which opened up directly into their living space – I think that scared them a bit, as people from the street could just walk in.'

This cramped living did not last long: with the help of friends, they moved to a slightly bigger place in the Rivierenbuurt, and then to a ground-floor flat a few streets away in Waverstraat. It had a larger bedroom with access to a small garden, which Beauty appreciated – she missed her gardening. Fezekile and Beauty shared the double bed.

Jacqueline confirms – and I cannot help laughing at this – that 'During her time in the Netherlands Fez started many projects but did not necessarily finish any.' Vintage Fezekile. 'It was always fun being with Fez. When she was around, something happened. That also made it a bit tiring sometimes, as she was always up for something new.'

Fezekile and Jacqueline's biggest adventure was a few years later, when volcanic ash from Iceland's Eyjafjallajökull grounded air traffic. Through their network, they received news that a Kenyan mother, on her way to Canada for her daughter's graduation, had found herself stuck at Amsterdam Airport Schiphol. She had lived her whole life in the countryside, and spoke only her mother tongue and Swahili. Language was not her only barrier, however – she had no money to buy food during her unplanned layover.

Without knowing this woman, off Fezekile and Jacqueline went to the airport with money and food. With hundreds stranded, many of them Africans, locating their target was a mammoth task in itself. With only a name – Sophia Atila Kafu – and a photo, they begged security to let them through and help them find her. Fezekile was in her element – according to Jacqueline, 'She loved these kinds of things.' When they found Sophia, Fezekile switched easily to Swahili. They connected Sophia to her daughter in Canada; suddenly, her awful ordeal seemed bearable. It took a couple of days before passengers could leave, but at least the Kenyan mother had food and euros.

The early Amsterdam days were filled with nervous energy and anxiety. Fezekile was happy to have created distance between herself and the country that had hurt her so deeply. The One in Nine Campaign was formed specifically to support her. It did an amazing job. But she still did not feel safe.

Her priority, when she arrived in Amsterdam, was to try to obtain asylum. Igna Oomen, a human rights lawyer assigned to her case, advised that Fezekile and Beauty would have to provide a letter showing that they were not entitled to police protection should they return to South Africa. They also had to provide newspaper clippings and detail incidents in which they had been threatened with any harm during the trial. The authorities, she was advised, may argue that the danger had dissipated after the trial. So, they had to find evidence that, even after the trial, there were plans to harm them.

Fezekile informed Oomen in an email that:

> Since we left there, the youth league has asked that I answer to the country about who I was working with, that I could not have done this alone. Since we left the ANC Ronnie Kasrils Minister of Intelligence (who is considered to be in the Thabo Mbeki camp) has been called to a disciplinary action to account for his communication with me around the rape. The rape that is seen as part of the conspiracy. Never mind that I actually called Uncle Ronnie first as an uncle and elder.

It stressed Fezekile that she could not gather all the information she required herself, because she was out of the country. She relied on friends and the One in Nine Campaign in particular. She mentions the people who supported her: Shaun, Dawn Cavanagh, Carrie Shelver (a gender activist from People Opposing Women Abuse (POWA) and one of the founders of the Tshwaranang Legal Advocacy Centre and the One in Nine Campaign), Delphine Serumaga from POWA, and Thokozani Mtshali, a journalist and friend who she says was sidelined at *The Star* newspaper for covering the

Fezekile in exile in Amsterdam, October 2008

story in a way that was deemed sympathetic to her. During her stay at the safe house she had sent text messages to all of them about feeling unsafe. At one point, she had written in her diary, she believed that 'the crime intelligence people were in the camp out to kill us'.

It was clear that she anticipated difficulties with obtaining proof about the danger they faced, and was mindful that she had lost some friends by daring to take Zuma on. She wrote, 'outside my family/NGO people, hard to know who would be on our side really, so that limits the numbers'. It was communicated to the NGOs supporting the asylum application that this was a very delicate case diplomatically; in the end, asylum was not granted – Fezekile could not commit to the process and its requirements.

A new life began, but Fezekile was always terrified. Every time she received a call or inquiry from a journalist, she panicked. Some wanted to interview her or write books about her, but she always declined. She was, however, determined to rebuild her life.

With her magnetic personality and adventurous spirit, she became

Fezekile trying out make-up, which she never wore,
in Amsterdam in October 2008

active in the cultural and NGO scene. She worked for Aidsfonds and the Koninklijk Instituut voor de Tropen (Royal Tropical Institute, or KIT), an NGO that supports civil society movements and programmes that 'improve health and ensure equitable social-economic development', according to the institute's website. It provides research, training and education mainly for countries in the global South. KIT also has a gender office. This was right up Fezekile's alley; she immersed herself in her work, becoming popular with her colleagues.

Fezekile loved to keep busy and had a hunger for knowledge. During her stay in Amsterdam, she enrolled for a short course at Vrije Universiteit Amsterdam. Her confidence grew in leaps and bounds when she was asked to contribute to a course on HIV/Aids and speak to students about her life as an HIV-positive woman at the Wageningen University.

She had the master's students whom she addressed at this time eating out of her hand. She was popular with local and African professionals in Amsterdam. And, it was during this time that she developed a love for teaching.

She loved to dance and sing, and spent many afternoons and evenings attending local festivals and poetry evenings. In front of a live audience, she performed her now-famous poem 'I Am Khanga'.

'So, tell me about the kanga,' I'd asked.

'What about it?'

'Well, you wrote a poem about it?'

'No, dear. I wrote a poem about it *after* they had made the kanga a big deal. Up until that moment it was just a piece of cloth.'

While in witness protection, Fezekile had written a letter to her 'darling sister Hlabi'. The letter was a message of love and defiance in which she rejected Zuma and the court's meaning of the kanga. It would mean what she wanted it to mean, she wrote: 'I wear my Khanga with no panty underneath.'

She had never imagined that the kanga would be a symbol of seduction, she told me: 'Don't people wear lace and satin and G-strings when they want to seduce someone?'

'How would I know?'

We had a great laugh – knowing, however, that the debate about what rape victims were wearing when they were raped is anything but frivolous. (Until the day she died, Fezekile could not grasp what the obsession with her kanga was. She just could not see it as anything seductive: it was a long piece of cloth that mothers used to carry their restless babies on their backs, or women wrapped around their bodies at the beach. It was long and wide enough to cover the entire body, with minimal flesh exposed. She did not see how a kanga could be construed as an invitation.)

Her life took on a manageable rhythm and she continued seeing a therapist. But, after four and a half years, Beauty was not coping. She was in her late sixties and desperate to return to her roots. The weather was harsh. She hated being away from her friends and family. Fezekile could not bear to see her mother unhappy and approached Shaun and her friends in the One in Nine Campaign. Again, they used their contacts to connect her to Marc Wegerif, an anthropologist whom they knew from his work with Oxfam. Marc's wife Teresa Yates is an American-born lawyer who is now the Legal Resources Centre's deputy director. Together, they opened their home to Fezekile in Dar es Salaam.

'Fez was the kind of person, you meet her and it's like you have known her forever,' Teresa tells me. Everyone was family; if someone showed her some warmth, she returned it tenfold.

Before moving to Tanzania, Fezeka came for a visit and stayed with Teresa and Marc for just over a week. During that time, Teresa learnt that Fezekile was very close to getting an EU passport, which, she felt, would open a lot of doors for her. Fezekile mentioned the language barrier – to obtain the passport, she would have to pass a Dutch test, a task she deemed too difficult. And the winters were harsh, and Ma was depressed, she told Teresa – who challenged her by saying, 'You have been there so long, an extra year will not hurt.'

Every time Teresa and Marc gave her a reason to prolong her stay in the Netherlands, Fezekile countered with a reason why she could not. Teresa laughs as she remembers how Fezekile frowned and said, 'And then I would have to also do some menial jobs.'

Teresa responded, 'If it were me, I would get that EU passport. It would enable you to travel and explore other opportunities anywhere in the world.'

But Fezekile was adamant: she and Ma had to leave Amsterdam. She returned to fetch her mother and their belongings. They headed for Dar es Salaam and stayed with Teresa, Marc and their two daughters for over a year. Later, they found a place not far from Teresa's and the two families continued to see a lot of each other. But, in 2011, Beauty wanted to return to South Africa.

Fezeka called Ivan Pillay and told him of their unhappiness. Ivan promised to assist and called Moe Shaik. Moe promised to speak to Zuma, who had become president, and guarantee their safe return to South Africa.

This is absurd. Fezekile could not just return to her home, the democratic South Africa for which her father had sacrificed so much. There was no law forbidding her from entering South Africa, yet, as I have argued, the law is but one signpost as we negotiate our lives.

Moe returned a message to Ivan, presumably from Zuma, informing him that Beauty and Fezekile could return to South Africa and nothing would happen to them. Such power! And such blindness to its reach!

Fezekile believed they never stopped watching her, that they knew her every move.

'Who is "they"?' I asked.

'The rapist's people. They always know where we are and what we are doing.'

Fezekile claims that, shortly after they sent word that they were keen to return home, she sensed that she was being followed. This told her it was not yet time to return to South Africa. 'We did not know where to go, what we would eat, who was still a friend, a relative, you know,' she said.

Some of their friends were also not persuaded that the risks had dissipated, and advised Fezekile against the move. But she wanted to make her mother happy, and told me that she felt guilty about uprooting Beauty.

So, for the first time in five years, they touched down on South African soil.

While Fezekile was helping Ma to settle, local government elections took place in South Africa. She says her friends dragged her to a voting station to cast her ballot, but she found that there was no record of her. I asked her about this, whether it was not simply a matter of her not being registered to vote in that particular municipality. She insisted that she had registered there, and felt strongly that was something sinister about the omission. This was all the indication she needed that South Africa would never welcome her back.

'So, it must have been a setback to see that, while you were fighting and making progress, others had erased your existence anyway?' I asked.

'I'd been fighting all my life dear. All my life. It wasn't anything new. I was coping, sometimes not coping, one fool at a time dear. Always one fool at a time.'

She packed her bags and headed back to Dar es Salaam, where she found a teaching post at an international school. She was not qualified, but had such a natural flair for teaching that the school was willing to bend the rules and hire her. She taught there for almost two years; Dar es Salaam was constantly looking for English teachers, so there was demand for her skills. She stayed with Teresa and her family once again.

Teresa says this was quite a happy time for Fezekile, and that her daughter Zora adored Fezekile. Marc and Teresa's older daughter, Maya, was at school in the US.

In Tanzania, she also met Eileen Moyer, to whom I reached out without success. Fezekile had enormous respect for her and, from what I can gather, she is a formidable academic and has worked as a research manager and coordinator of the 'Anthropology of AIDS in the 21st Century' research group. I understand she and Fezekile later talked about writing a book together. Generations must know of Fezekile's valour. Future young feminists, in particular, must be able to draw from a rich and

Fezekile in Dar es Salaam

well-resourced pool of chronicles about Fezekile's life; I welcome all initiatives to document it.

But then, the classic pattern emerged again. As soon as things started to go well, Fezekile wanted to leave. Her restlessness would not leave her alone. Perhaps exile had made the constant need to move a part of her DNA. It was the only life she had known – things felt wrong when she was at rest. When she had no reason to move, she created one.

She became unhappy at the international school. The people around her recognised her teaching potential, and she was surrounded by private schools that were constantly looking for English-speaking teachers. Fezekile was at the right place at the right time. Teresa found her a job as a librarian at a small school.

'Kids loved her. She could go into their world, like she did with Zora. She could go into that imaginary world and enjoy it and not feel uncomfortable in it at all,' Teresa recalls.

She also did some arts and drama activities with the children at this school. They were thrilled with the gumboot-dancing classes – there would be much laughter and noise as the children performed their moves and chanted at the top of their voices. Whenever a teacher was away, Fezekile was called in to substitute.

'She was also looking at doing some correspondence courses through Unisa,' Teresa says. But she did not have a matric certificate.

The restlessness came once more. She complained that she was not really doing what she was passionate about and that the classroom, not the library, was where she belonged. Again, Teresa told her that the opportunity would come, and that she needed to remember that she did not have the necessary qualifications on paper. She was luckier than most people in that she had the opportunity to work in a school environment. Keep working, Teresa advised.

But Fezekile kept searching for another reason to quit. This time, she said the culture of the school and the uniform of the teachers were making her feel like an outsider.

'So, what are you going to do?' Teresa asked.

'I don't know.'

Teresa came up with an idea. Because Fezekile was so great with Zora and knew how to connect with her, Teresa thought they could design a programme that would keep Zora in a mainstream school even though she had Down syndrome: 'I wanted to keep her in an inclusive environment and she had been in one in South Africa and had been doing well. I wanted to carry on with that. But the schools in Dar were not so open to it. Children with learning disabilities, like in many countries on the continent, are kept at home or the parents send them to a special school where they are not really learning. They teach them basic things like dressing themselves.'

Zora could dress herself, Teresa says. What she needed was to learn.

Finally, they found a small school for Zora, where they hoped Fezekile could work as an assistant to meet Zora's needs. The school was hostile to the idea, however, because Fezekile was neither qualified nor Tanzanian.

Fezekile then got a job at Genesis School, a Cambridge International School. Her class C visa allowed her to do voluntary work. Soon, another school called, offering her a job as a second-grade teacher.

'So, she had what she said she wanted – a job as a teacher, working with children, being in the classroom,' Teresa says.

Things were looking up for Fezekile – the first academic year went extremely well, and she was thriving. Her social life was abuzz with friends from all walks of life. Her days were full – music concerts, poetry sessions and even an aerobics class (although these did not last very long).

Until, out of the blue, Fezekile came to Teresa and said she wanted to stop teaching Grade Twos. The school was developing an after-school arts programme – dance, drama, painting – and *this* is where she belonged. Teresa asked why she could not do both – teach and participate in the arts programme, which was an extramural activity in any case.

But Fezekile was determined to quit teaching.

'But why would you do that?'

'Because I am good at it and I like it,' she said, referring to the extramural arts programme.

'But you said you like teaching and that is what you are doing now?'

Yes, but she did not like that person and this person. Teresa told her that there would always be personality clashes at work, so she needed to be grown up about it and deal with it. Fezekile hated conflict, I have heard from many people. In the brief period for which we knew each other, I saw this in action. She wanted everyone to get along and would do and say whatever she thought she needed to for peace and harmony to be maintained.

Marc then pointed out to Fezekile: 'The thing about arts and drama is that when they run out of funds, that is the first thing they cut. These are not programmes that they have to have, but they have to have teaching.

Whatever happens at the school, they have to have a teacher.'

Fezekile responded that she had not thought about it like that, and recommitted to her work as a teacher. Thinking back, Teresa concludes that Fezekile showed signs of depression, although she did not recognise them at the time.

During her time in Dar es Salaam, Fezekile was on ARVs. There was a lot of fake medication on the market, so they tried the state hospitals and clinics. Teresa would accompany her to the local clinics for her medication and check-ups. She describes the experience as 'just horrific': the queues were long and patients would be called loudly to the front cubicle and asked personal questions in front of everyone. About five patients at a time would be asked intimate questions about their health. It was intrusive and outrageous, so they left.

'We went to another, smaller, hospital. That was better, although not perfect. But definitely better than the chaos at the big state hospitals and clinics.'

Then, Fezekile met a friend whose mother happened to be a pharmacist who got her all the medications that she needed.

Teresa says Fezekile was quite healthy, and had started swimming. 'She was a very good swimmer. There were people who helped her with lessons but it did not take long before she had mastered the art.'

She also went on a strict diet. A vegetarian when she arrived in Dar es Salaam, she became vegan. Teresa laughs and says, 'So just to make it more complicated, she then announced that she was going gluten-free, so no pasta, bread.'

Fezekile started complaining about her swollen feet and attributed this to the ARVs. Her CD4 count was good; quitting ARVs put her at risk of becoming ill. Again, Teresa was firm, telling her, 'You cannot go off your meds because your feet hurt.' There were no other side effects and Teresa says everything else was fine – there had been no test to show a causal link between her swollen feet and the ARVs. Teresa prevailed, and Fezekile stayed on the medication.

At that time, Fezekile was still bubbly and active on the social scene. She had a lot of fun with Teresa, Marc and some friends, often going on picnics and road trips. She seemed happy. She probably was, for a while. But she started talking about the urge to visit her father's grave in Zimbabwe. Teresa was concerned because it was before the end of the school year. As I listen to Teresa, it strikes me that, years later, Fezekile had not moved on from that position. A few weeks before she died, this was her plan – to quit work and do things with her mother, including visiting her father's grave. A message she sent me exactly a week before her death communicated her plan to do just this. She thought she would be strong enough to undertake this annual ritual.

Teresa and Marc told her, 'No, you cannot do that. Just get through the school year. You need to focus and finish what you started. Then, if later you feel like going to your father's grave, then great, it will still be there. You can go and visit, and tell him about your students, experiences. But don't walk away from something you said you wanted. This experience at an international school is great. International schools the world over are looking for great teachers. Don't walk away.'

Fezekile was persuaded, or so it seems – she carried on working. But, a couple of months later, she came up with a different reason for wanting to go. Her mother was struggling and sick, and she needed to be with her. Again, Teresa and Marc felt that she shouldn't leave her students in the lurch, and that she had to see the school year through. There was nothing wrong with Beauty – at least, nothing that could not wait until the end of the school year.

But then, Teresa and her family went travelling, giving Fezekile the opportunity she had been waiting for. While they were away, she returned to South Africa, packing only her clothes. To her credit, she sent Teresa a message saying she knew this is not what she wanted, but that she just had to leave. Teresa laughs now, but, at that time, it was not funny at all. She called Fezekile: 'I cannot believe you would do that. I cannot believe you just left.'

But there was nothing they could do.

Those were tough times, Teresa says. Fezekile did not have a job. It was only the charity of friends that kept them going.

In the meantime, Carrie Shelver travelled to Tanzania to pack Fezekile's stuff. Teresa expressed her disapproval to Carrie, saying it was not acceptable for Fez just to up and go. She said the same thing to Fezekile, and reminded her that she was no longer young and had to get her act together. Over the phone, Teresa told Fezekile that she could not keep using her mother as an excuse to run away from things: 'I said Bee Bee [Beauty] is not always going to be here and, uh, so you need to find something for yourself.'

Teresa was particularly concerned because, even after Fezekile returned to KwaMashu, she did not stop complaining. She hated being there. She wanted to be in Pretoria or Johannesburg, but her mother insisted on staying in Durban and Fezekile did not want to part with her.

'So I said you came to South Africa to take care of Bee Bee, and you need to be somewhere where you can work so Bee Bee needs to follow you. Bee Bee must follow you to Johannesburg or Pretoria, if that is where you find work. Because you need to do that,' Teresa tells me.

Teresa was right to be hard on Fezekile. It is one thing for people to have been supportive and sympathetic when she was younger, but as a woman who had entered her forties, and with the rape trial becoming a distant memory, she needed to reclaim her life. It was nearing the sunset of Zuma's presidency. The further he retreated from the public scene, the more likely it would be that the memory of Fezekile would also fade and, with it, the goodwill she had experienced. Teresa and Marc felt strongly that that the best way to fight back would be for her to build a solid and stable life. *That* would be a real story of triumph.

'I did not know her during the trial but for me, you could just see so much potential. She was so smart, so energetic. You just wanted to see that spirit survive. For her to be successful at something, anything, just focus,' Teresa tells me.

In 2015, Teresa and Marc moved to Johannesburg. Fezekile was happy at this time, and had found a job as a teacher at Tree Tops Primary School in Musgrave. Even here she was lucky – so many qualified teachers do not find jobs, especially in cities of their choice. She was on the verge of qualifying as a teacher. Her experience and positive disposition had got her the job – the job she wanted to quit shortly before her death. She was particularly lucky. Not only had the school hired her, but it had also offered her and Beauty rent-free accommodation in a massive house in Musgrave.

Fezeka had informed me that, after getting her driver's licence, she was keen to sign on for a sign language course so she could work with an organisation that supported families with deaf children. Just three weeks before her death, she told Teresa about her plan.

Again, Teresa asked her: 'But what about your job?'

'No, I can do both. I can work during the day and do my training and home visits in the evenings,' said a confident Fezekile.

Teresa saw Fezekile at the end of August 2016. She was clearly not well. Teresa does not know when she stopped taking ARVs. 'She never would have told me when she made that decision because she knew I would disapprove,' she says.

Teresa's question was bold: 'You look terrible. What is going on?'

Fezekile laughed and downplayed the extent of her deterioration. 'I have been a bit sick. Nothing serious.'

'Are you taking your meds?' Teresa asked.

Fezekile lied.

'How is your CD4 count, then?'

'It's been a bit low, but it will pick up again.'

People have a right to refuse treatment, but, given Fezekile's wide network of friends who were there with her in her darkest hour, who picked her up and supported her constantly over many years, I wonder whether there could have been some intervention when she started deteriorating at the end. She loved and trusted so many people; I wonder whether, collectively, there could have been an opportunity to persuade her, just as these people had managed to advise her and persuade her in other major decisions in her life.

Teresa goes surprisingly quiet when we delve into Fezekile's last days. She was told that Fezekile had several clots – a common occurrence among HIV-positive people – and that doctors could not operate. Teresa and Fezekile had kept in touch on the phone prior to that, which is how Teresa learnt that Fezekile was on antidepressants, which she told Teresa were probably responsible for her swollen leg and nausea. Teresa advised her to ask her doctor about that and to request that they change her antidepressants if they were making her so ill.

'Look, she did not share everything with me because she knew I would push her to go into a hospital and get proper care. I accept that Fez did not let me into her space in that last week. She would have known that I would not just accept easily that she was not at a hospital.'

Teresa pauses. Then, 'I have made peace with that because she knew that when she needed me, I would have been there. She knew I loved her and that there is nothing that would happen that would make me walk away. So ...'

She does not complete her sentence.

. . .

'I want to let you know that there are people who loved her, and loved her dearly, and we will support your efforts to celebrate her life.'

I am moved when Danielle continues, 'Whatever you need to make this happen, I want you to know that you have support all over the world.'

Her voice breaks.

Danielle Callaway and Fezekile had an intense relationship. Danielle, from Washington, had been living in Dar es Salaam for three years. She and Fezekile met in Dar es Salaam when both were at a crossroads, trying to figure out who they were. Beauty was back in South Africa, and Fezekile had returned to continue her life. It was about 2012.

Their hearts found each other. When they were together, Danielle says, their spirits opened up to each other and shared the abundance of life. Her eyes well up as she wonders whether she should have been more accessible to Fezekile in her last days. I comfort her, knowing that when Fezekile's heart connected with another's, nothing broke that bond – not time, not distance.

Danielle is full of energy and passion. She respects what Fezekile represents politically, but feels very strongly that she cannot be reduced to politics. 'As important as that was to her and South Africans, there was more. Does that make sense?'

'Yes, it does,' I assure her.

'I was going through a transition and she was always going through a transition.' We laugh – that was Fezekile, always on a journey, always starting a new journey without necessarily completing the previous one. 'We were both what each other needed. Her energy was so refreshing, it was magnetic. I learnt so much about myself when I was with her.'

Danielle did not have a clue who Fezekile was, why she was in Dar es Salaam, and what circumstances had led to her departure from South Africa. She had simply met a young, beautiful, curious and bubbly person and their souls had spoken to each other. On long drives and walks, they spoke about everything. I learn for the first time that Fezekile contemplated having children. She thought about it hard and wondered if it were possible – if it is something that would have made her happy. She was in her late thirties; it is not surprising that she had reached a 'what next?' phase of her life.

'It was little things that defined our life together. I told her, I said Fez, you *have* to sing. You *really* have to sing. Your voice is a gift and so many people have tried to take away that voice of yours. You *have* to sing.'

Soon thereafter, Fezekile started voice training and singing lessons, which Danielle happily paid for. Until the end, Fezekile would send Danielle photos of her singing in a choir in South Africa.

But Fezekile was Fezekile. Soon she was jittery again, looking for the next exciting and urgent project. They disagreed a lot about this: Danielle is focused and hardworking, with clear goals and a road map of how to achieve them. She is a master of corporate life.

'We'd be on the singing and teaching, and she would talk about something else that she wanted to do.' She says this without any malice or impatience, just the pure indulgence of someone who loved Fezekile.

Something else happened to Fezekile during her time in Dar es Salaam: she learnt to talk back. Her passion was reinventing her body not as a war zone, where men had fought their battles, but as a beautiful, sensual and authoritative part of her being. In a daring shoot, she posed nude with a calabash on her back. Her back is turned from the camera. We do not see her face, just her silhouette, but her formidable presence fills the space. Her hips and bottom are prominent; she is clearly posing, proud and formidable, with her arms raised. It is a triumphant image, confident, cheeky. She is striking back. The calabash represents Africa

Fezekile in her element, singing and performing in Dar es Salaam

because it is a uniquely African object, a symbol of the melting pot of African cultures.

Danielle tells me this was Fezekile's favourite image. She loved to share it with those close to her and revelled in the power she commanded in that image. It truly is a moment of victory – a death of shame and subservience, but a rebirth of sorts. In this image, she reclaims her enjoyment of nakedness and reasserts the power of her body.

Danielle was also concerned when Fezekile went off her ARVs, and encouraged her to keep taking them. She told Danielle that she hated how they made her feel – that she was always tired, which she hated.

'She was strong-willed and knew what she wanted and was always honest, so honest about what she felt and wanted. I expressed my opinion without undermining her wishes.' We pause again as the memory of their life together brings tears to her eyes. She recovers and says something that perhaps reflects Fezekile best.

'She believed in happiness and joy. She believed that, when she was happy and joyful, it would boost her immunity, that happiness and energy have an effect on our health. She was determined to work towards attaining full happiness. Every day, she did this.'

Fezekile, a believer in the power of the universe, a believer that every good deed would be rewarded by another good deed and all she had to do to 'fix' her life was to be happy, honest and generous.

In the end, Danielle would return to Washington and then Nairobi.

'Fezekile had so much going on emotionally,' Danielle says. 'There was so much that she was unsure about and she was never really sure about what she wanted to do, or how to get there, and she was never really happy when she got there.'

Everything with Fezekile was some kind of crisis, she recalls. Even when she was enjoying life, there was always some kind of crisis. 'There'd be periods when everything was kind of okay, and then there'd be a crisis.' But she admires Fezekile's fighting spirit and her fervent belief that life was worth living and fighting for.

Danielle had a pair of designer gumboots that she loved to wear. When she left to return to Washington, she asked Fezekile what she would like to keep as a memento of their friendship. Fezekile chose the gumboots. They were a bit tight, but she wore them when she performed for her pupils and friends.

The two communicated regularly. Whereas Fezekile informed Danielle about her health, Danielle did not believe she would die: 'She loved life way too much. She was a fighter. And a communicator. Fezeka would not go quietly into the next life. She would tell all of us, all of us who loved her, if she thought she was dying. I have to believe she came into my life for a reason, a season, and I have to be satisfied with that.'

. . .

A final voice joins the chorus of Fezekile's Dar es Salaam connections – Allan Mapundi, the young, charming farmer who became her soulmate. I remembered that Allan had come to visit Fezekile in Durban in August 2016, when her emotional and physical health had been waning. Carrie Shelver had been instrumental in bringing Allan to South Africa; she smiles warmly when she talks about Allan and, from the naughty glint in her eyes, I suspect there was something far more than friendship between Fezekile and Allan. Beauty voiced a similar suspicion.

When Allan left Durban, Fezekile fell apart. He had to return a couple of weeks later to help her gather herself. It was on the eve of his departure in late August that she told me she was dreading the days ahead and was on the verge of a breakdown.

They were introduced in 2008, by a close mutual friend whom Fezekile had met in London. Allan says they developed a sense of family and community when Fezekile's niece, Nokuzola, and Beauty eventually joined Fez in Dar es Salaam in that same year. They spent a lot of time together, taking long walks and drives. 'I was her guide everywhere she went,' Allan says.

When Fezekile returned briefly to the Netherlands, the two of them stayed in touch. 'We e-mailed each other a lot, several times a day, telling each other everything.' Over thousands of kilometres, their affection deepened. 'She was my everything,' he reminisces sadly.

Life took on a happy, blissful beat when Fezekile returned to settle in Dar es Salaam. He confirms that the two of them started dating officially. 'We became more than good friends, beyond brother and sister. We talked about everything.'

They would see each other three or four times a week, go to movies, and just talk, Allan says. Eventually, he would spend nights at Fezekile's place. 'It was a happy time, we were happy. She would dance and sing. It was beautiful.'

But sometimes, when Fezekile was angry, she would shut him out and need time alone. Allan remembers that there were times when both Fezekile and Beauty would become melancholic about their forced exile. Fezekile was working, making friends and hanging out with Teresa and Marc, but would suddenly become sad about her mother's pain. 'MaBeauty always said she was so tired of being in exile for the second time after spending her lifetime fighting for South African independence,' he recalls.

Fezekile tried to make the experience less painful for her mother by organising visits to Swaziland and Botswana, so that Beauty could see some of her relatives and the friends she'd made during her first exile. But she continued to miss South Africa. While Teresa remembers that, after Ma left, Fezekile had absconded and returned to South Africa, Allan's version is, 'She had to fly to South Africa and leave her job in Dar es Salaam to come stay in South Africa to be with Ma.'

It seems Fezekile returned to Dar, but left again. She was not particularly concerned about her future and 'believed she would succeed in becoming a kindergarten teacher, while having fun with them at the same time'.

I ask Allan whether Fezekile ever talked about Zuma and the trial. 'Yes, we talked about it, she told me a lot about it. But sometimes she completely wouldn't want to talk about it. It ruined her psychologically.' He also remembers how very careful she was in all her movements and could not shake off the feeling of being watched and followed. 'But she still lived life to the fullest,' he assures me.

When Fezekile returned to South Africa, she was even more jittery about her safety but still determined to live. She could not afford much, so making security arrangements seemed like a luxury. 'She always feared about her safety. And seeing [Zuma] almost daily in newspapers, TV, hearing people talk about it on the radio, it really disturbed her,' he tells me.

Now that Fezekile is gone, Allan wishes he had stayed longer during his visit in August. I remind him that he did return when Fezekile needed him, and she knew she could count on him. He was very concerned about her health; she was losing weight. 'My concern was that she was losing herself, she was struggling with Ma's health condition, seeing Ma suffering with memory loss, Alzheimer's and so on. It was a difficult time but we tried to do fun stuff as well.'

They would go to see a movie, walk to Fezekile's school nearby, go grocery shopping. 'We couldn't go far because we were with Ma most of the time and Fezeka herself had a tight schedule, from work, choir practice, driving school, choir performance and so on.' Allan is describing the Fezekile that many have described: always on the move, planning the future, changing her mind, but always in search of something new. He believes she had a lot to live for and that taking care of her mother was her priority.

Allan continued to raise his concerns about Fezekile's health, but she would brush him off, saying, 'What doesn't kill you only makes you stronger.' He continues, 'Her priority was not her health any more, she was concerned with Ma's health and she was always very afraid of losing Ma and not having anyone, especially from her family, to support her closely. She dreaded the day when Ma would depart.'

He goes on to recall, 'Fez knew how to interact with everyone. She shared her love with everyone and was a very strong woman. Regardless of what she had been through, she was always smiling, making jokes.'

Five months after Fezekile's death, Allan is in pain. There is palpable sadness as he remembers the moment he learnt about her passing. It was the evening after she died. He was driving in Dar es Salaam and had stopped briefly at a red traffic light. His phone rang. It was Langa, a mutual friend, asking if he'd heard the news.

191

'I completely froze,' he says. 'I had my cousin, my uncle and aunt in the car. It was just few metres from my place, but I had to drop my aunt and uncle two kilometres away. I never said a word, drove all the way there, dropped them, don't recall even saying goodbye to them, didn't get off the seat and drove all the way back to my place. As soon as I got in the house, with my cousin I started crying out loudly, and he was wondering what happened because I never explained a word to him. I was so devastated.'

Allan could not attend the funeral, and continues to mourn. 'I am still in devastation. Sometimes I don't believe it, I feel like she is just in South Africa and we haven't communicated. Without her I feel empty, for me it will never be the same without her. We always stayed in touch. We always felt near to each other.'

I ask him if he has any hopes of being strong again.

'I don't know.'

. . .

Back in South Africa, how was life unfolding for the accused in the trial's aftermath? Had the trial had any influence on his behaviour?

I had many face-to-face interactions with Zuma when he was the country's deputy president. I was a journalist at SABC Africa and he was the main mediator tasked with ending the civil war in Burundi. I interviewed him a number of times on my television show, *Today in Africa*, and had various briefings off air with him. We had plenty of discussions, over tea, about the struggle, the future of the continent, our families. He loved his children and always asked me about my family, which comprised only my brother and my mother. My mother was a nurse in Scotland. He would ask me regularly if she was well,

A collage of images of Fezekile put together for her funeral

if she was happy. On one occasion, he phoned my home when my mother was visiting. I wasn't there; he left a message that Zuma had called.

'Zuma?' my mom exclaimed. 'Which Zuma?'

'*Yena uqobo.* (The real Zuma.)'

My mom was positively charmed. She told me that he was so kind, asking her about her life in Scotland, telling her that South Africa needed her skills and that she must return home. He mesmerised her when he told her she had done a fabulous job of raising me.

His anecdotes about exile life were entertaining and educational. He was always the perfect gentleman, never flirtatious or inappropriate – polite, courteous and a great conversationalist. I was very comfortable with him, and admired his commitment to our country and the continent.

Until he suggested, one Saturday afternoon, that next time, I must come not just for tea, but for dinner and breakfast. I have never been alone with him since.

In the week that Fezekile died, I received a call from a senior journalist who had covered Zuma extensively and had been allowed into the nucleus of the Zuma strategy. They had developed great rapport over the years as she covered the country's explosive developments. There had been many off-the-record briefings, just as I had had with Zuma and many other newsmakers. She had been to his home to interview him about sensitive news matters. Nothing unusual there: journalists all over the world do this. She had covered the rape trial and, like many others, had given Zuma the benefit of the doubt, buying his story of a political conspiracy. There was so much happening around Zuma at that time – he had been fired as the deputy president of the country, and rumours of corruption plagued him.

The journalist concerned did not feel uncomfortable at all when, after a meeting with the South African National Editors' Forum (Sanef), Zuma invited her to his house to discuss a sensitive matter in front of one of his trusted aides. She was exhausted and wanted to get home but, when she realised that a top aide would also be present at the meeting, she thought it may be a story of national importance that could not wait. Reluctantly, she drove to Zuma's home in Forest Town – the same home that Fezekile had visited on that life-changing night.

After a few minutes of conversing about nothing in particular, Zuma called the male aide aside for a private conversation – she did not check which room they went to. They returned after a few minutes and the male aide said his goodbyes. When Zuma asked the journalist to accompany him to another room as he had something to show her, she did not think much of it – the same had just happened with the male aide. Not being familiar with the rest of the house (beyond the entrance, dining room, lounge and study where they had met previously), she had no idea where he was taking her. She followed him; he opened the door to a room and she stepped inside.

It was his bedroom.

Before she realised what this all meant, he had his arms around her, was pressing himself against her body, and planted a long, determined kiss on her lips. Her back to the door, she froze for a moment as his tongue invaded her mouth.

I don't know why, but I was shocked. Not *that* journalist, who was regarded as the authority on Zuma's inside circle. Perhaps, for him, there really weren't any no-go areas. As a journalist, I was familiar with her work and could not imagine why Zuma would see her working closely with him as an invitation for a sexual relationship.

There was a long silence between us as she put her face in her hands and cried. That day, she told me, she realised how it had happened to Fezekile: 'I knew it. I did not believe her before and thought Zuma was a victim. But that day, about three years after the trial, I knew she had been telling the truth.' The burden of her silence had weighed heavily on her. It was cathartic for her, finally, to say, 'I believe Fezekile.'

She managed to pull away from Zuma and said the first thing that came to her mind: 'I am on my periods.'

He loosened his grip and stopped kissing her. He was smiling, warm and friendly. Bizarrely, he reassured her, telling her not to worry because they could try next time: 'He gave me an almost fatherly pat on my shoulder, telling me not to worry.'

She was too stunned to make sense of what had happened. She replayed the many years for which she had covered and interviewed him, the many conversations about newsworthy events – some private and some in the presence of others – but could not make sense of this moment. In my house that day, about a month after Fezekile's funeral, she cried. I let her.

'Now why did I do that? Why did I say I was on my periods instead of saying no? Why did I not say no?'

Had things gone further, would a court of law have ruled that the encounter was consensual because she had not uttered the word 'no'? This is my point about the law: it does not accommodate the range of emotions that human beings who are shocked, frightened, stunned and mortified may exhibit and the reactions that these emotions produce.

'When Fezeka died, I heard you were writing her book and I just had to speak to you and tell you this. My silence, my guilt, I had to express it. I've been asking myself, why didn't I speak out?'

'Why do you think you did not speak out?'

'So many reasons: my family, Zuma's position ... and I covered the trial. I saw how brutal it was, the total humiliation of Fezeka and her mom, I did not have the appetite for it. The easiest thing was to just block it off. Who would have believed me, anyway?'

Fezekile back in Durban, in declining health

She did not have the energy, she said, to explain how she had ended up in his room, let alone his house. She had been seen at his news conferences, interacting warmly and respectfully with him. 'So, who would have believed that Zuma had taken advantage of me?'

She called a friend who, at that time, was close to Zuma, and told him what had happened. 'He totally freaked out and said he can't fucken believe this guy. After all of that?!' But he also made it clear that he could not deal with this – he was too close to the inner circle. And so, the chapter closed.

Why now? Why say this now? Because, if we are to give Fezekile a voice, then more of us who have witnessed Zuma's predatory side must back her up. If we are to declare 'Remember Khwezi,' then we must do so boldly, courageously, honestly.

It was staggering that, a few years after the rape trial, Zuma had not become more circumspect and had given in, again, to his impulses and had not heeded Judge van der Merwe's warning in his judgment:

It is totally unacceptable that a man should have unprotected sex with any person other than his regular partner and definitely not with a person who to his knowledge is HIV positive. I do not even want to comment on the effect of a shower after having had unprotected sex. Had Rudyard Kipling known of this case at the time he wrote his poem 'If', he might have added the following: 'And if you can control your body and your sexual urges, then you are a man my son.'

Perhaps this is part of the problem: that Zuma's rapacious drive is seen as an 'urge', and not as the violence that it is.

CHAPTER 8

'Every day feels like death now'

Back in South Africa, Fezekile's life took a difficult turn.

Towards the end of her life, she was stressed and traumatised by another person whom she had trusted and allowed into her life.

In July 2016, my phone rang in the early hours of the morning. It was about 3 a.m. I was awake anyway – the last stages of pregnancy can keep a woman awake for hours, battling discomfort and a constantly full bladder. I always put my phone on silent when I sleep and would have missed Fezekile's call had I not seen the screen flashing.

Calls that come at that time can only spell trouble. I answered, petrified. I was convinced that something had happened to her mother. Fezekile was hysterical.

'She attacked Ma. Chased her around the house with a knife.'

'Okay, just breathe. Breathe. In an out, in and out. Okay, let's count to ten.' We actually did – one, two, three, four, into the phone, she in Musgrave, Durban, me in Johannesburg.

'What is going on?'

I could not believe what she was telling me. Fezekile had got herself into serious trouble. She had married someone, a Zimbabwean national, the previous month – June 2016 – to help this person get South African citizenship. Her wife's name was Thandeka Asheley Nyasha Makuku. She had not talked to anyone close to her before making such a life-changing decision.

The two had met in 2015 when Fezekile was in Zimbabwe to visit her father's grave. She had stayed with Thandeka. It seems their relationship was toxic and violent. I could not make sense of everything she said that night, but did grasp that Thandeka 'had anger issues' and was refusing to leave Fezekile's house – even though they had agreed that she would do so after getting the marriage certificate.

What I did not quite get was the full story of how the altercation between her mother and her wife had happened, and how Thandeka had ended up chasing Fezekile's sick, elderly mom around the house with a knife. Fezekile wanted to end the marriage and get the woman out of her home. I advised her to go back to bed – that I would think about it and ask my lawyer friends for help. I woke to a text message from her: 'What action to take dear sister? I just need to spread the word. This is an awful situation.'

I felt sorry for Fezekile, but could not help also feeling slightly irritated. How could she have got herself in this situation? After everything she had been through – the betrayals, the financial difficulties – how could she have opened herself up to so much harm? Thandeka was a virtual stranger.

The marriage stressed her so much in the weeks that followed that she expressed fear for her and Beauty's safety. She genuinely believed that Thandeka would not stop until she had destroyed her. Every time I spoke to Fezekile about the conflict, she would become agitated and unsettled.

She wanted to end the marriage behind Thandeka's back – she thought that if she told Thandeka that she wanted out, Thandeka would harm her and her mother. The marriage certificate had not arrived yet.

Until this certificate was firmly in Thandeka's hands, Fezekile felt that she could not get rid of her.

There were many text messages from a highly strung Fezekile. She confessed to 'not thinking straight because she had not slept or eaten well in a while'. She said she was 'trying to get cash to buy food and extra linen and fill the house with people while she [Thandeka] is here. Also want to get Ma out of it'. After numerous conversations, I determined that Thandeka seemed to feel rejected by Fezekile – whereas the intention of the marriage had been to secure South African citizenship for Thandeka, she wanted them to be truly married. She was reeling from Fezekile's telling her that she was not available for a romantic relationship with her, let alone a marriage. This is Fezekile's version, at least.

'She was getting so possessive and clingy,' Fezekile said of Thandeka. 'I am a free spirit. I cannot be controlled like this. Anyway, one fool at a time, dear.'

I asked a friend who is a judge to advise on the best way to annul the marriage, then e-mailed the information to Fezekile. When she learnt that her spouse would still need to be informed, she called me. She seemed to be falling apart on the other side of the line.

'Okay, okay, okay, so I am basically stuck? I am trapped? I don't need this. I really don't need this.'

With hindsight, I know it was not fair to kick her when she was down. But I had to ask: 'Fez, what were you thinking, *mara*? How did you get into this manure?'

She didn't answer, but chose to laugh at my use of the word 'manure'.

In the early hours of the following morning, I could not sleep again. The first thing I did at sunrise was to send her a message asking if she was still breathing. She responded: 'It is morning and my thoughts are back on Thandeka and the marriage. I want to keep the peace but it is cruel to let her go on believing she will get the marriage certificate, when I plan to annul as soon as she leaves. I don't know what safety measures to put in place. I don't know if I can annul without her participation? What if she retaliates?'

Fezekile had taken to bringing different people to her home to create a veneer of safety. She believed that Thandeka would not harm her or her mother in the presence of others, but that she and Beauty were vulnerable alone. But this was not without its challenges either: one of her messages during this time read, 'Having a hard time transporting people back and forth to come sleep here. Others didn't pitch. Am so on edge. Eish.'

A couple of days later, there was another violent encounter with Thandeka. I woke up to an SMS: 'It's ON. The war.' According to Fezekile, Thandeka had threatened to be her biggest nightmare and that one of them would leave the house in a body bag. 'I am so alone in this horrible Durban,' Fezekile said.

Typically, Fezekile wanted as many people as possible to know about her marriage and help her get out of it. She sent messages at any time of the day to any person she loved and trusted; many received her cries for help. Some from her past were still there, supporting her and trying to help her get herself out of this mess.

It seems Carrie Shelver ('truly wonderful and I love her', according to Fezekile) was working this case. Carrie is one of those people who quietly supported Fezekile behind the scenes for over a decade, without seeking glory for doing so. She, too, was receiving those late-night messages. With her legal background, it seems she was able to help. One of her strategies was to bring Allan from Dar es Salaam to Durban.

Shortly before Allan arrived, Fezekile sent me a message she had received from someone who seemed to know Thandeka:

She is in serious problems. She bought a car in Zimbabwe in April 2015. She never put the car in her name. It turned out that this car

202

was involved in a robbery. Someone was killed. She cannot prove when she bought the car. The police arrested her and she was on bail after one week (November 2015). I helped her out with rent etc., since she claimed she was not earning a lot of money on a tour with artists in Australia. Her contract with donor for LGBTI work was not extended. Later I found out that she has never been in Australia. It is a whole range of lies and debts to dozens of people. She had to go to court again earlier this year but she fled to Zambia … My last information was that she had no income and friends in Zambia. Likely facing a long stay in prison. Try by all means to keep her far from you. If you know where she is let me know. Since she is gone, I don't think she will continue threatening you. But if she does please inform me. Stay far away from her.

Fezekile's lack of judgement here was jaw-dropping. From what I can gather after Fezekile's death, in addition to Carrie's intervention Auntie Bunie played a role in knocking sense into Thandeka. Whereas it does not appear that the marriage was ended, Thandeka left Fezeka and Beauty in peace – but the saga had taken its toll.

These were serious allegations that Fezeka was making against Thandeka. I approached her, using an intermediary, in the hope that she would agree to speak to me and give me her side of the story. At first she was open to the idea, but soon afterwards declined, stating unequivocally, 'I would love to have NOTHING to do with Fez … or any of her friends. I would really appreciate if you stop contacting me too.'

I asked Fezekile how her life might have turned out had these events not taken place.

'I just hate that people took advantage of me,' she replied. 'That their lives went on, you know. That Ma and I are the demons who must live and die in poverty. That their power continues. I don't think I would be living like this if my life had not been disrupted. I was starting to feel like I belong with people, that a big family can claim me as one of their own.'

Then, an admission: 'I have not allowed myself to say that he stole from me, because somehow, it made him win, you know. If somehow I blamed him for stealing the life I had before, saying so, makes him, I don't know, win somehow.'

'But do you think he *did* steal something from you?'

'Yes, he did.'

In the three months before she died in October 2016, her emotions were all over the place. On 14 August, she performed in a church choir concert in Durban. I was meant to be there, and had booked my flight and accommodation. I had expected to give birth in early August, but the baby had a mind of its own, coming just three days before the concert; despite my initial insistence on attending the concert, things just did not work out that way.

When I had told her I would be there, she had messaged, 'Wow! Perfect timing. I really needed to hear this now. Thank you. Just came back from rehearsal then a crazy outdoor concert. Was completely entertained. And now I feel loved, appreciated and strong vs the weak confused stupid self I felt earlier. Day is ending well!! PLEASE PLEASE PLEASE come baby!!!'

I assured her that we all feel weak and confused sometimes. It is not a crime, I said: 'Cry if you must, forgive yourself, don't imprison yourself. It will be okay.'

Her response was doubtful: 'It does not seem like it will ever be okay. Not for me. Never for me. I need to find someone to cry with. Don't do the whole crying alone thing. Doesn't work for me. And I can't wait for therapy on Thursday. Hmm.'

It was a very difficult decision for me to make. In the days before the birth, and even while I was in hospital, Fezekile sent me incessant text messages asking whether the baby had arrived and whether I'd be able to come, and telling me what an honour it would be to have me in the audience. I'd wake up in the morning to, 'Has the baby arrived? Girl or boy?' The next morning, it would be, '*Sana* dear, eat all the right foods, meditate, bring that person to earth!!'

I felt pressured, but did not want to let her down. I raised her hopes by insisting that I would do whatever it took to be there. The baby arrived at her own chosen time, though – 10 August, too few days before the concert. In the end, I was content to receive a text message from her telling me that performing in the concert and singing in the choir had been 'an enriching experience': 'It lifted my soul and made it soar. I loved it,' she messaged. I was glad that she had had this moment of glory, comfort and validation.

Lungi Dlamini, her childhood friend from Swaziland, says Fezekile was a real performer at the concert. Unlike the other choristers, she did not have her music in front of her, but it was clear that those many evenings of practice had stood her in good stead. She was in her element; as the others turned their pages and followed the words and notes, she sang straight from memory – and from her heart.

She had thrown herself into choir practice, which she attended in the evenings after work. She was also taking driving lessons. These activities were an escape from the chaos of Thandeka and her domestic life.

Then, just as suddenly, she would fall off the wagon. She became agitated that someone had used her real names in a Facebook post. The person had meant well, though, and had paid tribute to her and reminded South Africans not to forget her. Sometimes it was so easy to forget that, behind her bravado and colourful personality, her fear of being found out and compromised was real. There was a court interdict against the use of her name; South Africa's media had respected this for ten years.

'I am surprised that someone would use my name now,' she said. 'But I am too tired to feel anything. I am just tired.'

'What would you like me to do? I could make a public appeal, on Twitter, reminding people about the interdict and asking them not to use your name because it is hurting you?' I offered.

'They say he isn't hiding so maybe I shouldn't.'

'What do *you* say?'

'I think that I should be the one to give permission to use my name. They shouldn't be. Make the public appeal.'

'What are you afraid of now? You know, if your name gets out there, what do you fear?'

'His supporters are crazy. Very crazy. They could harm me and Ma.'

'Even now? After all these years?'

'A close comrade of his told me that he bears grudges. He does not forget. I know he has always known where I am. But you know ... maybe ... *ag*, I don't know. I mean, what's in a name? People could harm me, yes they could.'

It did not seem appropriate to remind her that she had said she was ready to come out, that she would be at the book launch and reclaim her name. But her fear seemed real. She may have seemed confused, but she appeared, always, to have a sense of being watched and knew that many people did, indeed, know her name and her whereabouts. She still felt safer using the protective layer of her alias.

In the end, I decided not to make the public appeal; it would only draw more attention to her. I left it, hoping it would die a natural death.

She was also anxious about her driving test. With her life adrift, she still did not have a driver's licence at forty-one. She was not ready for the test and did not have money for more lessons. She was fretful about her mom's well-being; added to that was her sudden unhappiness at work. In a previous conversation, not so long ago, she had said to me,

'Working with those precious souls gives my life meaning.' Here she was, so close to achieving her teaching qualification, wanting to quit, all because she had not secured the one day off a week that she had requested.

Of her teaching career, she said, 'That was the initial plan anyway. But Ma lost her words and I was shattered. I dreamt of magic money from the sky and just writing and spending time with her for six months. Couldn't have that so I instead asked to have Fridays off so I can spend time with her. Today, a month later, they responded saying no.'

She felt that the best option would be to resign. This would be a bad move, and I told her as much; she wanted to leave the following month, when the third school term ended on 23 September.

'What will you do for the rest of the year?'

'I will spend the rest of the year with Ma. Do lovely things and visit places, places that we both love.'

'But surely you do not need to leave your job, Fez? It is too risky. Is there no other way you can spend time with her without compromising your job? And, if you leave the school, you will have to find new accommodation and disrupt your lives again.'

'I feel sad that for her the last ten years of her lucid life have been filled with so much loss and trauma. It breaks my heart.'

'Honey, I know, but quitting work will create a different kind of problem, which will give you a headache and something else to be sad about.'

'Of course it is a contradiction, because without the little R6 000 I earn and rent-free living, I won't be able to afford a place to stay, let alone to take taxis to the park or museum or visit friends' places of her childhood ... But I feel like I am drowning. I need this time with her.'

What created this sense of urgency in Fezekile was an incident at the bank in which her mother had been unable to remember her PIN.

At the same bank, Beauty had not been able to recall her own signature – according to Fezekile, she simply had not known how to sign the withdrawal slip. 'I broke into tears right inside the bank,' Fezekile said to me. 'The staff thought I had received some bad news, like death or something. Dearest, every day feels like death now.'

Her demons were demanding. She confided the same information she had shared with me to Wisani, a childhood friend with whom she had grown up in Swaziland. Months after Fezekile's death, Wisani and I realise that she had confided in a lot of us. Wisani says, 'She had this ability to speak to you and make you feel that you are the only person in the world for her, the only person in whom she trusts. Such drama!'

Fezekile had also told Wisani, 'I so badly wanted a honeymoon with Ma before she is really lost to me. It has been so fucking hard. Have felt alone. Need to leave Durban. No support here. Little. Challenge is Ma regressed. Been hoping that she would hang in there till we settle again and can have peace. And she is so restless. Wanted her last memories to be happy. Feel cheated and so sad that time has been stolen from her, from us. She is anxious about security, having no family and friends, having no home, leaving me with nothing ...'

This sounds like a Fezekile who believed she would outlive her mother. Her tone, her constant reference to Beauty's mortality, made it seem so imminent. That is why I was surprised when I met Beauty. Her mind may wander from time to time, but she showed no obvious signs of ill health. She was fit and lean, with a glowing complexion; from what I gathered from Ntsikelelo (the nephew who lives with her), Bule (Ntsikelelo's daughter, who visits practically every day) and Lungi, Beauty's moments of lucidity far outweigh those of confusion. In a few conversations I had with her in the aftermath the loss of her daughter, she described in great detail how she felt and remembered events from the past. I did not get a sense that this was someone who was knocking on death's door.

Wisani also believes that Fezekile and Beauty needed a break from each other. On numerous occasions, she had invited Fezekile to visit her for a week or two. The response would always be, 'What will Ma do without me? I cannot leave her by herself.'

But, in a cruel twist of fate, Beauty *did* end up alone. It is Fezekile who left her; only time will tell what she will do without her child.

I had tried my best to dissuade her from quitting work without securing new employment. I even advised her not to rush her decision – to consider unpaid leave and return to work as soon as she had achieved her goals. This was not a decision she had to make, in the end.

The last few weeks of her life were surreal. For years after the trial, no one had mentioned her – then, suddenly, in August, she was on everyone's lips. August is women's month in South Africa, which went some way towards explaining the renewed interest in her, but this had been the case in each of the ten years since the trial. Even Julius Malema – the feisty, militant leader of the Economic Freedom Fighters (EFF) – was talking about Khwezi. He wanted to apologise to her for the comments he had made during and after the rape trial. Malema had been a staunch supporter of Jacob Zuma, a man for whom he had once been prepared to die, during the trial. About Fezekile, Malema had said in January 2009, 'Those who had a nice time will wait until the sun comes out, request breakfast and ask for taxi money. In the morning, that lady requested breakfast and taxi money.'[29] He was taken to the Equality Court, which found him guilty of hate speech in 2010.[30]

Zuma and Malema's parting had been dramatic and acrimonious, their mutual hatred becoming as intense as the love and loyalty they had once shared. Malema has since conceded that backing Zuma was a mistake, and that he had seen the error of his ways. Many believed him, especially since he and his party have scored major victories in exposing Zuma's corruption. But many others were sceptical, believing his Damascene conversion to have born from expediency – had the ANC not expelled him, they maintain, he may never have apologised to Khwezi. Fezekile was not impressed. On 18 August, almost two weeks after the silent 'Remember Khwezi' protest staged at Zuma's local government elections speech on 6 August, she sent me a text message: 'Just heard Julius Malema apologised to me on Power FM [a local radio station] and is looking for my contact details to apologise to me in person. Never a dull moment ...'

'How do you feel about that?'

'His sorry is cheap. Have had enough contact with crazy people to last me a lifetime, thank you very much.'

In the same month, on 23 August, Kasrils won his lawsuit against Kebby Maphatsoe, with R500 000 awarded for damages and a ruling that Maphatsoe apologise publicly for saying that Kasrils had organised Khwezi as a honeytrap for Zuma. By this time, Fezekile was so detached that she did not even know this was happening, despite its making headlines. Excited, I sent her a message about it. She responded 'What? Where? When did this happen?' Knowing her financial situation, I had anticipated a different response. Wisani also sent her a message, telling her about the outcome of the lawsuit. She laughs as she recalls how blasé Fezekile had been: 'You know, Fez could just quit this world and be in her own universe.'

When I told Fezekile about the money, her first question was, 'Did he state publicly that the money would go towards Ma and I?'

'Yes. Why?'

She paused for a moment. 'Well, sweets. It is not that simple.'

'Geez Fez, I thought you'd be thrilled.'

'It's just that, you know, I was accused, I was portrayed as greedy, that I targeted the rapist for fame and money. So now ...'

'Oh, I see.' It is true: Adv Kemp's line of questioning had left one in no doubt that he was painting a picture of a 'loose' woman who wanted Zuma to support her by building a fence around her mother's house and financing her education, and that she was interested in writing a book – which, given Zuma's stature, would sell well. She could have written a book, but didn't. She had spoken about writing a book long before this saga, mainly to share her thoughts on feminism, life in exile and, most importantly, her father's role in the liberation movement. Since her departure from South Africa, she had been hounded by so many writers and filmmakers. As far as I know, she had not given a firm yes to any of them, but had agreed that some aspects of her life could be documented. Nothing concrete had come of this, until she had agreed to the book I wanted to write because we had developed a relationship of trust. In her words, 'I feel that the time is right.'

It was as if the country had realised it had unfinished business, that the story of this young woman did not end with the rape trial that saw Zuma acquitted of her rape. Without lifting a finger, Khwezi had forced herself on the public domain again and the sheer force of her presence reverberated everywhere. People were, for the first time since 2006, giving themselves permission to say, 'We believe Khwezi', or 'You may have been acquitted, but what you did was revolting and justice was denied to Khwezi.'

Fezekile was treated appallingly during the trial. Some of us spoke and wrote columns about this. The mob that had been organised to threaten her, burning her picture outside court, was in charge; those of us who supported her were outnumbered, at least publicly. I remember presenting my late-night radio show every day during the trial. Every night, I would get home battered and bruised. Long before Zuma's acquittal, a lot of male listeners had become emboldened, crass and vicious. I certainly hadn't declared Zuma guilty or innocent. But, as a talk-show host and commentator, I had criticised his conduct and questioned how

The silent protest on 6 August 2016 by four young women as President Zuma
addresses the nation in the wake of the 2016 local government elections

so many could look up to a man who, if he had not committed rape, had certainly committed incest and spat on the grave of his own comrade. But Zuma's supporters, male and female, had no time for questioning his moral code or demanding that he account for his behaviour. Khwezi was a slut, and anyone who raised his or her voice in her defence had to be labelled and shouted down.

After a torrent of sexist, abusive SMSs and calls to my show about

*Fezekile and Beauty at a Legal Resources Centre event to honour assassinated
struggle icon Victoria Mxenge, 27 August 2016, Durban Country Club*

'women who ask for it', I could barely remain intact. The misogyny was palpable. One particular SMS brought me to my knees: 'Women like you talk too much. You must be raped to be taught a lesson.' One listener sent me a threatening SMS, claiming to know where I live and giving my home address. I felt physically ill. My employer suggested I take a few days off to recalibrate. As Pumla Dineo Gqola writes, 'The creation of a public culture saturated with threats of violence also serves to silence dissent and strengthen the female fear factory.'[31]

But now, a decade later, the fear of speaking out about this case had dissipated. Her poem 'I Am Khanga' found its way into the media. The revival of her name and what she represented culminated in a dramatic, courageous silent protest by four young women who arrived at the election results centre in the capital, Pretoria, where Zuma was addressing the nation about the recent local government elections. They took their fight right to Zuma's face. During his address on live television, at an event attended by high-profile delegates including Cabinet ministers, foreign delegates, political party officials and the media, they did not sing, they did not chant, but just walked quietly to the front, displaying their placards: 'Remember Khwezi'. Zuma carried on speaking, seemingly unaware of this daring challenge to his authority and masculinity.

It took some time for everybody to realise what was unfolding: that four young black women, old enough to be his grandchildren, were confronting the president, with all his security around him, and reminding him that he was a flawed man – a man who had appropriated the body of his daughter and abused his power, authority and proximity to a vulnerable young woman.

These young women were there to remind him of that, rebuking him and all he stood for publicly – which is, to me, an often-violent masculinity that continues to thrive on its entitlement to women and children's bodies.

214

I travelled to Durban with my daughters and their nanny to ask Fezekile more questions about the book. My baby was only three weeks old. I was filled with anxiety because of a message Fezekile had sent the night before. It was sad, taut and desperate. It made me wonder whether she had ever contemplated suicide – something that had never crossed my mind in all our conversations. I do not know if her message was a cry for help or if it was just Fezekile being her usual, expressive self.

'Redi dear. I am a mess. My body is rebelling and my mind and soul are restless. Afraid my breakdown is REAL. Perhaps because I was going to crash anyway or it's been brought on by the fact that my friend Allan is leaving today and I don't know how the hell I am going to breathe let alone function. It all came tumbling down on me. I don't know what I'm going to do. I need that complete STOP Now. Just wanted you to know. Don't know what state I'll be in tomorrow.'

I didn't know how else to respond: 'Listen … feel it. You can't solve a breakdown. Give in to it. Walk into your darkness. But trust that the sun will shine again. Tomorrow will be whatever fate has determined. Tomorrow is not your problem.'

I was sad for her, but a recurring feature of her message struck me. There seemed, always, to be someone visiting, staying in her home, and departing, leaving her bereft. She had a constant need for loving company, a need to be with people who were on her side. What went on in her mind when she was alone? Were there conversations with herself that she was avoiding? She was full of contradictions. A complex human being – no surprises after everything she had been through.

I stayed in touch with her constantly, fearing she would harm herself. One of my text messages read, 'Hey dear, did you get through the night? Are you breathing?'

Her response was long and pained: 'Seems mad that I have to be reminded to breathe. Cried myself to sleep after Allan left. Then up at

1 a.m. head spinning so I bothered a few people with my thoughts so I could sleep. Woke up before 6 and immediately started sobbing and hyperventilating. I could not go to work.'

It dawned on me at that moment: in her testimony during the rape trial, she had told the court that, a few days after laying the rape charge, she had read in the *Mail & Guardian* that Zuma had said they 'had had a relationship of a sexual nature'. In her testimony, she says she found the idea extremely disturbing – 'and as a result of that I had an episode that my family and I, we call it the attack, it is not quite a fit but I just go totally still and I cannot move and my heart rate goes a bit low and I sort of get saliva bubbles out of my mouth. It has not been diagnosed as an epileptic fit but I just totally, I go still and it happens when I am in shock or emotionally upset.' She had also told the court about the negative impact that stress has on her CD4 count. Her medical records in the days following her laying the charge show that her health was suffering.

Auntie Bunie rightly intervened. My instincts told me that Fezekile was not in the right space to talk about the book, especially about events that had caused her intense pain. But I had let her down by missing her concert; I did not want to cancel our visit, in case she felt she needed me. But Auntie Bunie knew better, that Fezekile would not cope; we decided to cancel our scheduled conversations that week. It was the right thing to do. The focus now was on giving her a reason to travel slowly to the other side of her breakdown, where the sun shines and where she would feel strong.

Darkness approached as my family and I drove around Durban looking for a hotel. It was too late to fly back to Johannesburg with a hungry three-year-old and a wailing three-week-old, unused to the moving car. I could not answer my phone, which rang incessantly. When we had got settled, I took a moment to check it: fourteen missed calls and an explosion of messages.

She wanted to meet so that my trip was not a waste. I discouraged her, saying it was late at night and not safe to come out. She could not have slept well that night; again, I received messages from her throughout it, about her feelings and fears. She told me she had some documents to give me and that I should collect them in the morning.

I did. The box contained her diary, some notes she had made, and medical records and tests from before and during the trial. There was also a list of people to whom she thought I should speak if I wanted to tell her story.

I was relieved to receive a message two days later. She was cheerful, because 'Atha came from Joburg Tues and today and Aunt Bunie arrived when Atha left. Aunt Bunie is here so it's a great help. Feel a little lighter since she got here.'

From here, it seems she was taken to a private psychiatric hospital in Durban, which required a R15 000 deposit. There was no bed for her; she waited a week for one to become available. After admission, she saw a psychologist and psychiatrist and was put onto anti-depressants. There are some conflicting stories about who paid for what, but some say they sent her some money, which she combined with her 'moving and deposit money' to pay for her stay at the hospital. But, she said, 'Soon as bill exceeds that I will have to discharge myself. Nowhere to borrow and beg.'

We had discussed some financial matters pertaining to me writing her story. I reminded her of that and offered to advance a substantial amount of money to her for her hospital bill, but she told me she would rather not return to work and live off that money instead.

'I also want to move, maybe, to Dar es Salaam or Pretoria, so whatever you have will come in handy for that. Keep it for that.'

And then, 'Hi dear, just sending you a message before I hit rock bottom. The doctors say I will be stoned for apparently another week and it

217

will take another five for the anti-depressants to kick in. Love and light.'

I called her, but she did not answer.

She discharged herself when she ran out of money. I did not know that until after her death. She left Wisani a voice message that Wisani shared with me when we met about a month after Fezekile died: 'Have you ever heard of a disaster? An absolute disaster. I came back from hospital because I ran out of money.' She has a coughing fit. 'And they are still asking me for more. And to top it all off, my whole leg is sore, sore, sore, excruciatingly painful. And it is swollen, so swollen."

She then thanks Wisani for sending her money, but must already have left the hospital.

Wisani says Fezekile was down and that, with hindsight, her voice messages sounded like a cry for help. Wisani has known Fezeka for a very long time; her name features prominently in Fezekile's witness-protection diary. They also stayed in touch during her second exile. 'Maybe a hospital would have been a better place for her. Maybe being surrounded by more people who knew and loved her may have been better.'

It would have been at about this time that Shaun Mellors and Fezekile spoke for the last time – near her birthday on 17 September, three weeks before her death. He sent her money to celebrate her birthday and she reported back to him that she had had lunch with her mom and looked forward to a walk on the beach. He had no idea that she was very ill and believes that even she underestimated how urgently she needed medical care. After her death, he raised some money and confirms that about twenty people in Amsterdam contributed to his effort. This speaks to Fezekile's popularity and the deep love that so many had for her. Hopefully there are people around to ensure that there will be some financial assistance for Beauty.

Shaun believes Fezekile had so much to live for. 'She was happy, she loved her school, she was determined to look after Ma. Fez would never choose to leave her mother alone. Fez would never choose to die. I would never believe that and until I meet Fezeka on the other side and she tells me she chose to die … then maybe I will believe it. That is not the Fezeka I know'.

His eyes well with tears. It is clear that he is grieving.

Her response to my birthday message was uncharacteristically terse and empty. I encouraged her, knowing she was in a bad space, told her to smile and laugh, just for a moment, and to give herself a pat on the back and say, 'This too shall pass. I am loved, worthy and deserving of a meaningful, happy life.'

Her response: 'Thank you, dear, you are so right.' This was a first. Fezekile did not do such responses – she was expressive, loquacious and self-deprecating. She loved to laugh at herself and once told me, 'I got my laughing-at-myself trait from my father. He was funny, loved children and we always did fun and happy things.' Later that evening, she sounded much better, having spent the afternoon at the beach with Auntie Bunie, Lungi and her mother. She sent me pictures of herself in a red tracksuit. She looked thin and grey and the smile didn't quite reach her eyes.

She died so many deaths in the forty-one years she was alive, yet always managed to resurrect herself. From our conversations, it seemed to me that her life was one long, bruising battle. As soon as she would catch her breath, another blow would land. I wonder if, in the end, she just gave up on a life that kept failing her. Yet many of those close to her do not believe she would do this. I did not know her well enough, or for long enough, but our interaction persuades me that these friends are right. She loved life, and would not readily or easily walk towards death and leave Beauty to fend for herself. My wish is that the next life, in which she believed, would treat her more gently than this one.

So, this is the only way I know how to honour her, to continue where she and I left off. To honour one of the many messages she sent me on 15 September: 'I love my father Judson Diza Kuzwayo, also known as Mthethwa. I started writing in 2001 because I didn't want him to be forgotten. So I do want people interviewed while they are alive and before they get dementia like Ma. So would love it if you did/started the interviews.'

In all our conversations, it seemed she was preparing for her mother's exit. But who knows what happened in her last few weeks?

September became October. On 1 October, a week before she died, Fezekile sent me a recorded message enquiring after my daughters. It was brief and sweet, just checking on me and hoping I was doing okay. We had not spoken for two weeks. I had sensed that she needed space and was finding life overwhelming, so I had backed off. It is difficult to care genuinely for the subject of a book and what she represents. Obviously, I wanted to ask her as many questions as I could. But, as strong and courageous as she was, she could break into a million pieces; picking them up was always an arduous task for her and those around her. Auntie Bunie had spoken at the funeral about the many crises Fezekile had faced, and how she would be left to 'clean up' afterwards. Fezekile had so many triggers that could send her straight into the abyss; certainly, she was in that space now.

I kept my response short, light and cheerful. She was very compassionate when I told her that Neo, my soon-to-be three-year-old, loved her new sister, but was testing our love for her and throwing tantrums. 'Oh poor baby, she is used to being the princess and now mom and dad have messed up her world,' she replied. She promised to call to wish Neo a happy birthday the following week, on 8 October.

We continued chatting, with her giving advice about my regaining my pre-baby weight. 'Ma says the best way is the old-fashioned way. Tie a tight belt around your tummy. Ma says it worked for her. The thing is, Ma is the only witness. I did not see her after she gave birth to me so I don't know about this belt thing.'

Then, she changed the topic and left me a series of voice messages. I have listened to them regularly since her death. They break my heart every time. It is strange how we interpret words. When I first listened to the messages, they did not seem like a cry for help – just Fez talking as she usually did about how she felt. Now that she is gone, they have taken on a different meaning, a poignancy. I replay her words, detailing how overcome she was by pain, how she could not decide what to do with her life but that 'that decision will take care of itself'. She was often overwhelmed by life, but would quickly bounce back, saying, 'Anyway dear, I will take it one fool at a time.' This time, she said, 'I will just go with the flow.'

And then she got serious, describing her condition. 'I am not feeling so hot. It's just … um. I think I am just still going through a rough patch and I must go with it, go with the flow. I don't know what is going on.'

I expected that, in typical Fezekile fashion, she would describe, in detail, everything that was happening to her, everything she was feeling. I assumed she was only talking about her emotional state. Even though she had been off her ARVs for a while, it did not occur to me that the physical deterioration had started. Apart from a case of shingles earlier in the year, the first time she had ever suffered from an HIV-related illness, she seemed to be in relatively good health. She was religious about her vegan diet, supplements and meditation, but clearly something was missing.

She proceeded to inform me that she had been in bed for more than a week because her left leg was swollen. But that she was trying to move her body, because 'My dear friend says it is important that I elevate my leg but also keep my body moving, and my heart moving.

221

She has given me this exercise. Some yoga stunt.' Several times a day, with the help of her mother she would get off her bed, lie on her back on the floor, elevate her legs and push her feet against the wall. 'It is just Ma and I in the house so getting off the bed is a challenge. I almost, almost fell on her and she is confused, doesn't follow instructions properly, and not too strong and doesn't quite know what we are doing. It was hilarious, actually ... huuu! Almost like a circus.' She was laughing in her voice message, but her laughter was the sound of the vanquished – as if she has come to terms with the never-ending cycle of suffering that has become her life. By this I do not mean that she had come to terms with her death, but just accepted the frequency of her chapters of drama and sadness. She still believed – at that time, at least, a week before she died – that she would get well. She was delicate, animated and self-deprecating, drawing me in so that I could almost picture her and her mom, wrestling on the floor, trying to get Fezekile back on her feet.

I asked if she needed anything, how I could help. 'Oh dear, where do I start. It is what it is.'

I checked on her every day, especially after the message she left me in which she expressed a desperation to visit her father's grave.

In the next message, she told me she was going to send me all her passwords. This did not seem strange to me at all, given that I was writing her book; I had become used to her innocence and trusting nature. I figured she was giving me access to some of her writings and musings.

I did not have a chance to acknowledge this message before she sent another one immediately: 'Today I miss my father Diza. Isn't that strange? It feels like he never left. I see him everywhere. Yet I miss him terribly. Am I weird?'

'Not at all,' I messaged back. 'I have been there. I think about my father often. But my heart no longer aches. The world was dark when he left it, though … but I am living.'

'Oh. All sounds so familiar. It just flipped over. But when I am asked how I cope with life, I say it is those foundation years. It always hurts, though. Sometimes at the most inopportune time. Even now.'

'What is hurting you the most, when you think about him?'

'I feel robbed dear. Just robbed. I look at the comrades and how they live, and I feel robbed. Diza would not recognise so many of them.'

'Which ones in particular?'

'Ah, the looters, the corrupt, the arrogant, the rapists.'

We don't speak for a couple of hours; then, in the evening, she asks me, 'Have you ever wondered how a man becomes a rapist? Do you think they wake up and decide, today, I am going to be an arsehole to a woman? I mean, are they born rapists, do they become rapists, do they think about it or, you know, spur of the moment? That's been on my mind. What do you think, dear?'

On 2 October, she left me a voice message that she was coming to Johannesburg on the fifth. She was breathing heavily, her pauses just too long between each word. 'I am just sick and tired and I do not know what is next. Anyway there is something in Joburg, on the fifth, sixth, seventh, eighth and ninth, this holistic healing thing. Ummm, anyway dear, I don't know how I am going to get on an aeroplane.' She had told me that her leg was swollen 'from [her] bum to [her] toe'. She took a deep breath. 'But it is important that I go. And Auntie Bunie believes that I, I'll be better when I get there. So, let's see, it is in two parts. The spiritual and the physical.'

'What do you need?'

'I have tried everything, meditation, acupuncture, so let's see how this will work.'

Somehow, with her swollen leg – a suspected thrombosis – she arrived in Johannesburg. By this time, she was no longer answering her phone or replying to messages. The last message I sent her was on the fifth, the day she said she was starting her healing course. I told her that I had finally finished reading the transcript of the trial, and that I was proud of her: 'A bit broken, but I break many times over this subject. The system is entrenched. The point of my writing is exactly how the questions posed to you further entrench patriarchal and sexist views.'

The message remained unread; she deteriorated further. After all the battles she had fought and won – and fought and lost – she would not survive this one. When death came knocking at her door, I imagine her answering the door with her signature, 'One fool at a time, please.' I was deeply saddened, especially since her last messages were still full of hope.

Her last message to Lungi is heartbreaking. She tells Lungi she is in pain, but is getting through by visualising the two of them walking on the beach. She declares her undying love for Lungi and tells her she misses her. They had spent her birthday at the beach, laughing and snapping pics with Beauty and Auntie Bunie.

'Before she went to Johannesburg,' Lungi says, 'about a week before that, she was so worried about her mom. She wanted to get better for her.' This is why many struggle to believe that she chose death. She was depressed in the last few months of her life. Despite having taken her ARVs religiously for many years, she had stopped at some point, much to the disapproval of her many friends and activists in the HIV/Aids sector. She had chosen to focus on what she described to me as holistic healing. The opportunistic illnesses, combined with depression, made a toxic mix.

Of the medication she required to stay healthy, she had said, 'But it is costly. Sometimes I don't have money for the vitamins and supplements.'

'So what happens when you run out?'

'I get sick. Take time to recuperate and regain my strength. When my diet is good and my heart is happy, I generally regain my health. But stress is not good for my CD4 count.'

She had also started feeling that her life was not her own.

'What do you mean?' I had asked her some weeks back.

'I don't know how to explain it. I am feeling a bit strangled, suffocated ...'

I asked her whether she was happy.

'You mean now, or generally?"

'Both, I suppose.'

Her answer was revealing: she was constantly watching her back, wondering which thief was about to steal her happiness. 'Well, I am happy when I see Ma smile,' she said, 'but generally, I think happiness has a short life span.'

'What do you long for the most?'

'Ma's health, my health and peace.' The first two remained elusive; as for the third, I will never know whether, in dying, she attained it.

A week before her death, I sent her a message, saying I admired her fervent love for her mother. She was obsessive, wanting to protect Beauty from everything, including information about her thrombosis and her subsequent deterioration. But they lived together, shared everything with one another; I wonder whether – even with Beauty's lucidity coming and going, her difficulty being present and remembering what was happening – on some level, Beauty was aware that her daughter was quietly slipping away.

The two of them were admirable, always together, loving each other through exile, isolation and searing pain. But there was something pitiable about the dependency of their relationship. 'Oh, she is my world,' Fezekile told me. 'My father left me to take care of her. I have a clear picture at [Judson's] funeral of me holding her tight and consoling her and alternating that with rubbing her back. It's been like that for the past thirty-one years.'

It exasperated Wisani, who would chastise Fezekile and challenge her to visit her friends without worrying about Beauty.

What struck me the most was the deep sense of compassion that mother and daughter felt for each other. 'Ma suffered a lot,' she had told me some time ago. 'Her life was one of many losses. I mean, she waited in faith for a lover [Judson] to come out of prison. Then she gave up her acting and singing career to go to unknown worlds, just after losing her own mother. Then, after joining the struggle herself, losing the love of her life in exile, followed by losing her brother who she couldn't bury because it was too dangerous to return to South Africa ...'

She paused.

'I am not half as strong as her. She also had several miscarriages. Then she had to find out that I had been raped several times as a child, then the HIV diagnosis and then ... All too much, I tell you.'

.   .   .

She took her last breath, it is reported, on her way to a Johannesburg hospital.

Some of those close to her were surprised she had died, saying she had never been sick; others said she had been ill on and off for the better part of the year. I was not surprised that many told of times in her life for which they could not account. She confided in so many people all at once, but spoke to each one as if he or she was the only one who was there for her. I have no doubt she loved all her friends, who had become family. But I wonder whether a part of her enjoyed playing people off against one another – making them believe, individually, that she would not survive without them. She had the habit of appearing in, disappearing from, and reappearing in, people's lives. My observation is that she often told people what they wanted to hear and withheld information if she thought it would result in conflict.

Prudence Mabele seems philosophical about Fezekile's passing, accepting it as one accepts the inevitability of mortality. She does not judge Fezekile for coming off ARVs and feels that each must carry their own cross: 'We cannot impose our own solutions on people living with HIV. That would be the same as denying us our authority over our lives. She chose to come off them.'

Prudence pauses. 'But she did not choose to die. That was not Fez.' She raises her voice: 'That is *simply not Fezeka*. I will never believe it. Never. She battled with her emotions. All the time, she battled. But she was clear about one thing: her mother was her responsibility. She would never quit life and leave Ma to fend for herself. Never.'

Another pause, and a deep breath. 'And if she knew she was dying, if she chose death, she would never have kept those close to her so far away. She would have let us in.'

(I could never have known that the sun was also setting on Prudence's journey as we talked about Fezekile in a Rosebank restaurant. Mere days later, on 10 July 2017, Prudence – who lived with HIV herself – died of pneumonia. It is her turn, now, to be sent gently on.)

The days leading to Fezekile's funeral saw an explosion of news headlines. Every TV channel, radio station and newspaper wrote about 'Zuma's rape accuser'. They revived the trial as background material; some tried to editorialise her and look beyond the rape accuser narrative. Despite the intimate details about her life that the trial revealed, she remained an enigma. All people knew was that Khwezi had been forced to flee the country, and had settled in Amsterdam and, later, Tanzania.

For so many years, no one but the One in Nine Campaign had talked about Khwezi. Then, in 2016, the country that had stood idly by suddenly woke up. Activists, former Cabinet ministers, ANC elders, callers to radio stations chanted 'Remember Khwezi' or asked 'Whatever happened to Khwezi?' In their numbers, from their own private corners, they remembered the injustice visited upon a young woman by a man who, whatever the court found, had been a father figure to her.

But now, something certainly had come to pass. Indeed, Fezekile – Fezeka – is a Zulu word for 'it has come to pass'. Fezekile told me that her parents gave her that name because they did not believe they would be blessed with a child after struggling to conceive.

'Ma almost gave birth to me on the street. She was seven months pregnant and her water broke at night.'

'What was she doing on the streets at night?'

'No man, *dade*. Her water broke at home at night and her mother, who had been pregnant fifteen times, let her go to work the next day. You would think she would know better. While at work, she had contractions and decided to walk back home. I was born a couple of hours later. *Angazi* (I don't know). Seems drama was always there.' She laughed. 'Maybe that's why I like being up and about, being on the road. I was almost born on the highway in KwaMashu. Ma realised that she was still far from home so she turned and walked back to work and there a car eventually came and took her to the clinic.' She laughed again, enjoying herself and the drama of her birth.

Fezekile is no longer unmentionable. She is here. She has been all along, waiting to reclaim her home, her identity. Fezeka. That which has been fulfilled, completed, done.

It is done.

CHAPTER 9

Beauty

I find her on a Saturday afternoon, outside, bending over a tap and drain, washing pots. About four young men are in the yard, chatting and laughing. The smell of dagga is in the air. They receive me warmly. Beauty immediately stops her chores and leads me inside.

It is a small house in the township of KwaMashu in KwaZulu-Natal. The house is what is known as a matchbox, the small houses that the apartheid government built for black people in the townships. There are two very small bedrooms, a small lounge and a kitchen. The toilet is outside. Beauty walks in the dark, in the middle of the night, if she needs to use it.

The house is clean but neglected. The windows need fixing and the walls are crying out for a lick of paint. Because the rooms are so small, there is very little storage space. Most of Beauty's and Fezekile's pos-sessions – clothes, books, shoes, suitcases – are on the floor.

She is well, she says. But *'Ngi ya khathala* (I get tired).'

'Are you not lonely here?' I ask

'Not really. Sometimes. But I know people are very busy, they are busy.'

Ntsikelelo, Beauty's nephew, lived alone in the house for years. As a young man, he may not have prioritised things like curtains, cupboards, stoves and tiles, door handles – all of which need fixing or replacing. Yet, in these humble surroundings, Beauty seems to be at peace. She is content to be back home and feels a sense of belonging. She only regrets that the people she knew in her younger days, women and men her age, are no longer around and she is among younger people. She has lived in far more comfortable surroundings overseas and in South Africa. But she does not miss those, she says. She is tired of constantly being on the move and has no desire to leave.

It is a few months after Fezekile's death. Beauty tells me she cannot remember the funeral. But the void that Fezekile has left is there, every minute, every day. For Beauty, nothing can fill it. Not even her regular moments of disorientation can cushion her from this pain. It is raw and deep and there is no one to save her.

What makes Beauty's loss devastating is that Fezekile spent the better part of the past decade shielding her mother from life's blows. It pained Fezekile that Beauty had endured harassment and banishment during and after the trial. And, when they returned to South Africa after their second exile, Beauty would know no peace as her health and financial pressure took their toll.

Now, she has to face the remainder of her days without Fezekile, her pillar. I had long since decided not to interview Beauty because Fezekile had said she had lost her words. Even now, in the interests of integrity and because Beauty cannot always remember what she says, it would be incorrect to write things that she could not back up were she to be challenged.

Yet her nephew, grandniece and Bule don't believe she is as 'out of it' as it seems. They suggest I visit and speak to her. They are right. On that day, at that moment, she is surprisingly lucid as we sit down to talk. She even asks me to sign my book, into which she had put the programme

Beauty performing in a play

of the unveiling of Mandla Msibi's memorial. She remembers attending the service in Swaziland. There is a video of her, in the SABC archives, singing at the venue. Her eyes sparkle when she talks about her life as a dancer, singer and actress. Performing in Russia was the highlight of her career. From the dance stage, she made the progression to acting, appearing in 'numerous plays'. She remembers *Macbeth*.

Her proudest moment was her appearance in *Ipi Tombi*. The theme of the musical is apt – a near-replica of Beauty and Judson's life. A young black man leaves his village and young wife to work in the mines of Johannesburg. It was seen on the West End and on Broadway, and in Russian theatres.

'What do you love most, dancing, singing or acting?'

'Ha, do you think I can remember what I enjoyed most? Performing, *nje*, just made me happy.'

I have been warned that she loves speaking in her mother tongue, so

231

I ask my questions in isiZulu and she answers – not before commenting, 'So you speak Johannesburg Zulu. You speak well.'

She has written some poetry, and continues to let her pain pour from pen to paper. I am relieved when she says she wants her daughter's life documented. But she is uncomfortable. Since Fezekile's death, a few people have approached her, wanting to write about her daughter. It seems unfair to approach her now that the protection that her daughter once provided is gone.

Beauty was lucid enough, however, to decide where she wanted to stay after Fezekile's funeral – with her people at her childhood home in KwaMashu. She had travelled the world during her two exiles. But now, she wanted to settle down, even in these modest surroundings. To be accurate, her environment was less than modest; I felt, since I had told some part of her daughter's story, an obligation to find out whether she needed any assistance and to provide it – her house did not look suitable for an elderly woman who had gone through so much.

Some have expressed their doubt about Ntsikelelo's ability to take care of Beauty, given his unemployment and prolific dagga smoking. But when I visited, it was clear that the two of them were making the best of their situation. They loved each other – they argued, sometimes, but Beauty generally sang his praises. The neighbours did too, saying he was protective and made sure she ate well and took her medication. When they fought, though, they really fought.

Ntsikelelo had told me, 'She has moments of forgetting but she is okay. It would be good for you to speak to her so she knows what you are doing.'

I accepted the invitation. Beauty was expecting me, as Lungi had done the work of preparing her. I had to meet her: there is often fierce contestation over what is and isn't true, and books often result in family politics and squabbles. Opposing factions claim legitimacy and insist that their version is the true version; the writer gets caught in the crossfire. I could not countenance waking up to a headline that Beauty had not known anything about, or approved, the book. It would have soiled what was a beautiful project, driven by love and a deep belief in Fezekile's integrity.

I insisted that our meetings happened in the presence of Ntsikelelo and Lungi. I did not intend to interview her, just to ask her permission and tell her how far I had got. I made it clear to her that she did not have to sit through an interview, but she surprised me by saying she wanted to speak. And so, the stories about her life, travels and neighbours began.

We talk about everything and everyone, except Fezekile. In between, she loses her train of thought and pauses to catch her breath. We talk about life in exile and how the exiles had to be one another's family. She shows me photographs of the places she has visited – Russia, Geneva, London, Sweden. There are happy moments of her singing and dancing. And, on her wedding day, she and Judson smiling from ear to ear.

'Oh, here's "your handsome person",' I tease her.

'Oh? You think he was handsome? In isiZulu we do not say that men are handsome.'

'Come on, Mama. Really? Never mind IsiZulu. When you looked at him, what did you think?'

She just laughs.

She remembers places and points them out to me, followed by stories about her visits, what she did and why she was there. I tease her about a photograph of her, on her wedding day: with Judson smiling gently and looking on, Beauty has an earnest look on her face as she signs the register and binds her life to Judson's.

'*Ja*, you wanted to make sure you sign properly so he does not escape?'

She reaches out and squeezes my hand as she laughs. '*Ja*, me and, what did you call him? "My handsome person"?'

Beauty signing the wedding register while Judson looks on

'What was he like?'

'He was a hard worker, a family man. *Ja*, a family man.'

She says life was hard after Judson died because the movement didn't look after widows. I remember Fezekile saying the same thing to me. When I mention Fezekile's name, she says '*Ja, ja*,' and removes her

Beauty in Sweden with international anti-apartheid activists

glasses. She looks like she is about to cry. But she doesn't.

At the funeral, she did not shed a single tear. On our way to KwaMashu, Lungi mentioned that she would like to see her just let it all out.

She is angry, though. Very angry. If anger could break the body, it would have broken hers – there would be nothing left of her. Her anger is a seething fire that she has tried to control for years, but only managed to dampen its ferocity, leaving its flames burning softly.

'I asked a lot of questions,' Beauty says. 'About where we were going, where she was going. Even late at night, when she was not well.'

I do not know what this means so I keep quiet.

'The last days, I had no say. No say. No say.' There is a pause. 'Do I look ill to you?'

I don't answer, and allow the silence to stretch between us.

The softly spoken old woman is not about to lash out but, looking at her, the image of a pressure cooker comes to mind. There is turmoil, but she has denied herself permission to release it.

'When you are sick, it is not time to experiment, but who am I to speak?'

But then she says, 'Anything that saves life. We all must take it. If it saves life. But if it does not save life, then it is not from a good source.'

We are interrupted by a young man who walks through the open door. He puts some onions, tomatoes and notes – R50 and R10 – and coins on the small table.

'Did you forget the garlic?' Beauty asks and laughs.

'No, I did not forget it.' The young man puts another little plastic bag on the table. Beauty thanks him as he leaves.

'It is my turn to cook today. But Ntsikelelo is spoilt. Even when it is his turn, I sometimes cook for him.' There is no resentment in her voice. From her tone and smile on her face, she is happy to indulge him. But I am amused at the two of them, the elderly fragile aunt and the strong, young man, taking turns to cook.

'Can he cook?'

'Oh, he is good, very good,' she smiles, brightly.

After a brief silence, I take her back to the unpleasant topic. 'Did you expect Fezeka to leave? When you saw her getting ill, did you see it coming?'

'I accept. I accept. I just accept.'

'But you never saw it coming? You did not think she would leave you?'

'It will pass. It will pass.' She swallows hard, removes her glasses. It looks like she is about to cry, finally. But, in a split second, she finds her bearings, summons some strength and pushes the tears back.

'What was she like as a child?'

'Oh, she was an angel. An angel. From the start. You know, that child, an angel. If you did not have clothes, she would take her own clothes off and give them to you.'

And trusting. I see the same quality in Beauty now – there is no stranger anxiety or holding back. Mother and daughter, wearing their hearts on their sleeves.

'What do you miss most about her?'

She does not answer, and starts talking about something else.

'I just want to know. I just want to know. We cannot even fetch her spirit because we don't know where she died. We must fetch her spirit. It is the right thing to do. Her spirit must be fetched and Ntsikelelo is with me on that one.'

Ntsikelelo was adamant that the cleansing ritual must happen. It was long overdue. Fezekile had been dead for four months, yet nothing had happened. This ceremony usually happens after four weeks. For a dagga smoker, Ntsikelelo is very observant and respects traditions. Ancestors must be honoured. Like Beauty and many of Fezekile's friends, he was not sure where Fezekile died.

Unexpectedly, she starts to cry. I have been wanting her to cry but when it does happen, I am taken aback. I squeeze her hand and stroke her cheek with my other hand. We are sitting on a small, old couch in a room that is too tiny not to be rocked by her pain. *It's about time*, I think, but I don't say anything for a while.

'My mother lost a lot of children. There were fourteen of us at home and my mom buried some of us. Now, I am the only one left.'

'That must be hard.'

'Now I think about my mother and I understand. This pain, this pain. It is painful to lose a child. It can kill you. I have never felt anything like it. I was not prepared. I was not prepared. I was not ready. It is painful. So painful. You feel like there is something wrong with you, as a mother, if you allow your child to die.'

Our next visit does not happen. Beauty falls ill and is rushed to the hospital. She is disorientated and feeling weak. Lungi fears it may be a stroke. But, after careful examination, the doctors are certain there is nothing to be alarmed about. She is discharged and stays with Lungi for a few days. When they get home, Lungi decides to make her some scrambled eggs and toast. She tucks into her meal like one who is having her last supper. She was clearly hungry and may have suffered from hypoglycaemia after many hours, possibly days, of not eating.

Although she and Ntsikelelo have been getting along, he has a life that he was living long before she came along. It is not reasonable to expect him to be her nurse. Discussions about the possibility of Beauty being taken to an old-age home or care centre never really go anywhere, because there does not seem to be anyone available to make these decisions. People love and care for her, but she is essentially alone. In her old age, she is faced with decisions she cannot make – not just about finances, but the absence of some central point of command. It really is not clear who should ensure that she lives out the rest of her days in comfort. Nobody counted on Fezekile dying.

What complicates this matter is that Beauty has moments of lucidity and clarity of thought and argument. She can remember and relate events with precision, talk about the present and make commentary that is relevant and intelligent. Her wicked sense of humour comes to the fore from time to time. This makes it harder for anyone to take over; she wants to make her own decisions and leaving her family home in KwaMashu is out of the question, for now. She is resolute.

A few days after her health scare, Beauty travels to Kroonstad with her grandniece Bule. She has some family there and is determined to see them. Bule says she has never seen Ma this happy. There was a bounce in her step; she got up very early the morning of their departure, humming a tune and being very conversational. When they arrived in

Kroonstad, her family slaughtered a chicken for her as a welcome ritual and in deference to the ancestors.

'Ma was in her element,' Bule says. They stayed for over a week and Beauty was pampered and taken care of by her relatives.

I visit her on the anniversary of Judson's death, 1 May. My family and I were on holiday in Durban and drove out to KwaMashu to see her. She was looking good, but it was clear that the honeymoon with Ntsikelelo was over. The house was too small for the two of them. Bule loved and respected her father, but conceded that he was not easy to live with. A plan had to be found. It involved money; it was only fair that any proceeds from Fezekile's story go towards taking care of her mother. That plan is in progress.

I am reminded about what Fezekile told me in an SMS once: 'Ma needs to break with the past, in order to face the future, which promises health and well-being.'

I wondered who, between them, needed that advice the most.

'What does Ma want?' I asked instead. I received no response.

· · · · · · · ·

Epilogue

We walked steadily towards the altar.

It was decided that the pallbearers would be women, to mark Fezekile's commitment to women's rights. I had never been to a funeral where women had used their collective strength to carry one of their own. With my hand on that brown casket, it felt as if I was fighting for Fez, that I was picking her up after a nasty fall, that we were all saying, 'So many have let you down, but we will pick you up and carry you to a place of glory.'

We carried the casket up three flights of stairs and through a narrow entrance to the Methodist church. We mustered our numbers and physical strength to make a powerful statement about our presence as women and our rebellion against the patriarchy and violence that just would not leave us alone. We were drained, but had to fight for Fezekile. Many of us had tears running down our faces, but we had determination, strength in our numbers, and a raging fire burning in our hearts.

We were led in song – a powerful Methodist hymn, '*Ma yezenk' intando*', 'May Your will be done'. There was hardly a dry eye as we battled the heavy casket and our pain. It was at once a triumphant and harrowing moment, the opportunity to make up for all the times she had

240

been alone. But it all seemed so wrong, still. The unfairness of it hit me like a tidal wave. Every time Fezekile had come close to feeling her feet on the ground, it seemed to shift from beneath her. I found one of the verses extremely upsetting, and did not trust myself to lend my strength to carrying the casket.

My mind travelled to a conversation we'd had. Fezekile had been elated that the psychologist who was seeing her mother was pleased with her progress and that her mother had been so upbeat at the session, relating stories from the past. She sent me a video of her mother exercising and seemed amused by it. 'I have not seen this in a long time. The old girl still has her magic,' she said. And, 'Maybe life will work out after all, sweets.'

This is not how Fezeka was supposed to be buried, with appeals for a venue and funds for the burial and security. It was from the run-down house in KwaMashu that Fezekile's casket had made its way to the church. There was no shame in this, but it demonstrated the fact that, whereas many comrades – including those who had abused Fezekile and Beauty and rooted them out – were living lives of obscene luxury, at times Fezekile did not even have money for her medication. Fezekile and Beauty may not have gone to bed hungry, and had support from friends, but they needed financial support. They had been stripped of their dignity in many ways.

Zintle and Nokuzola had dressed Fezekile's body in a One in Nine Campaign T-shirt. Zintle believes her sister died of depression: 'It killed her. There was just too much happening in her life. It killed her. Nobody can survive that kind of life.'

Depression may not have been the direct cause of death, but it could indeed have led to major health problems like high blood pressure and a compromised immune system. Auntie Bunie and some activists from the One in Nine Campaign, women whom Auntie Bunie mentors and counsels, were with Fezekile in her last days in Johannesburg. Auntie Bunie was very close to Fezekile, someone whom Fezekile described to me as her 'mother and father'. She was a prominent figure, a mobiliser in women's movements, and had worked in exile in Lesotho and the Netherlands in particular to locate women's struggles within the liberation cause. She had been conscientised as a feminist and active in the struggle. Today, she continues to write about, and train young women in, feminist thought. She also identifies as a spiritualist. Fezekile adored her.

She spoke at the funeral, telling us that Fezekile had made a choice and had chosen the time and place of her death. This did not sit well with many of Fezekile's friends who had been with her before, during and after the trial. They referred to the voice messages that many of us had received a week before her death, where she had announced that she was travelling to Johannesburg for healing. Her friends believed she wanted to get better, and were not happy that they had not known the full extent of her deterioration in her last few days. Auntie Bunie's position at the funeral was that Fezekile had made specific choices and was very clear about whom she wanted around her in the end. This had to be respected.

As if to comfort her, the congregation, led by the One in Nine Campaign, sang, over and over, '*Fezeka we, thula mtwana mtanam, silwela amalungelo, Fezeka we* (Dear Fezeka, don't cry, be still my child, we will fight for these rights)'.

As I weep for Fezekile, I reflect on the smugness of her conquerors, the triumph of violent masculinities, knowing that they will live to traumatise another generation of girls. Khwezi did not die with Zuma's acquittal. While for many that was the end of the matter, it was the beginning of a different life for her and for other women caught up in the vortex of sexual violence, harassment and abuse of power in South Africa. I could not imagine any woman coming forward to accuse a

One in Nine Campaign activists surround Fezekile's casket

powerful man of rape after how Khwezi had been treated.

Khwezi's life is over. As the casket containing her mortal remains descends, I feel an overwhelming sadness for all the little girls, women and boys who will never know justice; who will constantly be asked why they did not scream, why they did not wriggle more vigorously from under their rapists' bodies, why they did not pull their hands away, why they did not say no a million times, why they are making up stories.

Fezekile had fought back. When I asked her where she found the courage to lay a charge against such a powerful person, she answered, 'I had to fight back. I have never fought for myself. If I don't fight back, this would keep happening to me. Even when it was clear that I would lose the case, I never once regretted fighting for myself.'

Fezekile was not entirely right. She did not fight for herself alone.

She fought for every one of us – every woman who has been too afraid to say, 'I was raped,' too afraid to say, 'That man groped me' or 'He demanded sex in exchange for the job, the lift, the favour.' She fought for all the women whose bodies have been appropriated by men, known and unknown, through lurid descriptions and graphic imagery – men who whistle and undress women with their eyes in public and private spaces. Uncles who wink at them when their parents are not looking, the managers and senior colleagues who, in a handshake, quickly turn their index finger to circle their palms, knowing that they will not call them out. That they are too paralysed to react. That, even when they are being disrespected, they will pull away quietly and carry on as if nothing has happened.

Fezekile fought for every single girl who has been in that situation. Dying so that many may live, she wrestled with political and male power. She lost, in the eyes of her critics, but not before inflicting a bruising wound. Not before demonstrating to the vulnerable that there is no shame in speaking out, even against the most powerful members of society. They may sing and dance for the cameras, be emboldened by the politics of spectacle, act like victims and gloat about their short-lived victories, but they have been unmasked. We have seen their true colours and are no longer afraid to stare them down.

Khwezi's was a moral victory. Now, she rests.

I watched MaKuzwayo. She was stoic, calm; she had a quiet presence about her. She is easy to miss, with her slight frame. But none of the trauma of the past decade and beyond is written on her face. One could say that she has aged gracefully. She is elegant and beautiful.

Throughout the funeral service, she was supported by family members – they held her arm, helping her move inside and outside the church. At the graveside, again, she was assisted. But surprisingly, like a bolt of lightning, she stood up and walked on her own, resolutely, to pour soil

With Beauty at Fezekile's graveside, just before the mourners dispersed

onto her daughter's casket. She walked so quickly, so determinedly, that she painted a different picture from the frail woman who had been held on either side by family members. I heard Zintle ask a relative why someone had not helped her. What if she had fallen?

To me, at that moment, Beauty looked powerful and steady. She had singularly brought Fezekile into this world, and seemed determined to be the first to commit her mortal remains to the earth. This was supposed to be painful, devastating for her. And it was. But it wasn't impossible, either. The same courage, fortitude and tolerance for pain that mothers endure when they bring life into this world may be at play when they bury their children. That is certainly what it looked like to me.

MaKuzwayo developed a certain infallibility as she poured soil into her daughter's grave. Or, perhaps, her mind had just shut down the pain

Fezekile's grave at the Stellawood Cemetery in Durban

and travelled elsewhere. I did not know. All I witnessed was a spritely woman who, at that moment, knew what was happening around her and got up at the right time to perform an age-old ritual. In a split second, she had said goodbye to Fezekile.

I spoke to her immediately afterwards, at the graveside when people were dispersing.

'I am so sorry for your loss. I wish you strength.' I spoke in isiZulu; Fezekile had told me that 'English irritates her so much sometimes'.

'*Kubuhlungu, kodwa ngi zo qina,*' she responded. It hurts, but I will be strong.

Farewell, Fezekile. Go gently.

· · ·

Fezekile Kuzwayo represented something much larger than the life of a young woman. She was not just Zuma's rape accuser, although that chapter should have been a salient one in the development of our nation. We should have learnt to interrogate the language of power. We should have walked away from her story with an understanding of the complexities of power relations and how they can destroy lives and contaminate the space for debate. We should have had a more cerebral and compassionate understanding about patriarchy as performed and lived by both the women and men who were intent on lynching Fezekile.

Women and children do not choose sexual violence, and its impact cannot be determined by those who have never experienced it or been vulnerable to it. Even if you doubt Fezekile's story, Zuma exercised power over her. He was her senior, her father's comrade and contemporary. He knew she longed for her father and constantly asked questions about him. He admitted that she was not emotionally solid. Even if she

Fezekile in Dar es Salaam. She had some of her happiest moments there

had invited him, he had a moral obligation to refuse.

Fezekile's childhood rapes are not irrelevant. At five, twelve and thirteen, how could she have been anything but a child whose innocence was stolen by those who should have known better?

We should have interrogated, as a society, our own tolerance for men who take without any thought for those weaker than themselves. We should have redefined consent and agreed that a weak person agreeing to a powerful person's advances, demands, or innuendos does not constitute it.

Fezekile deserved better. She lives. She inspires. She fights. Those who soil her name know, deep in their hearts, that their behaviour is predatory.

Leave your friends' children alone! Leave your comrades' children alone! Leave women and children alone!

Leave Fezekile Kuzwayo alone!

Notes

1 See http://www.sacp.org.za/main.php?ID=2326

2 News24 (2005) 'Shaik found guilty', News 24, 2 June 2005, http://www.news24.com/SouthAfrica/Archives/ShaikTrial/Shaik-found-guilty-20050602

3 A full transcript of the case as quoted throughout this book is available at the Johannesburg High Court: *S v Zuma* 2006 SA (WLD).

4 J Seidman and N Bonase (n.d.) '*Tsogang Basadi*: Finding women's voice from South Africa's political conflict', http://www.judyseidman.com/tsogang%20basadi%20paper.html

5 Truth and Reconciliation Commission, Human Rights Violations, Women's Hearing. CALS Submission: Dr Sheila Meintjes, 29 July 1997, http://www.justice.gov.za/trc/special%5Cwomen/meintjie.htm

6 For Modise's stance on the issue, as told to the TRC in 1997, see T Makgetla (2006) 'Zuma trial lifts the lid on gender-based violence during exile', *Mail & Guardian*, 17 March 2006, https://mg.co.za/article/2006-03-17-zuma-trial-lifts-the-lid-on-genderbased-violence-during-exile

7 United Nations (2016) *Special measures for protection from sexual exploitation and sexual abuse: Report of the Secretary-General*, 16 February 2016, A/70/279, United Nations General Assembly. See also N Cumming-Bruce (2016) 'Peacekeepers accused of sexual abuse in Central African Republic', *The New York Times*, 29 January 2016, https://www.nytimes.com/2016/01/30/world/africa/un-peacekeepers-central-african-republic.html?_r=1 and K Sieff (2016), 'The growing U.N. scandal over sex abuse and "peacekeeper babies", *The Washington Post*, 27 February 2016, http://www.washingtonpost.com/sf/world/2016/02/27/peacekeepers/?utm_term=.c381e3e7d4b6

8 For Rita Mazibuko's testimony (she is named Lita in the TRC document), see http://www.justice.gov.za/trc/special/women/mazibuko.htm

9 J Cock (1992) 'Women, the military and militarisation: Some questions raised by the South African case'. Paper presented at the Centre for the Study of Violence and Reconciliation, Seminar No. 7, 24 September, http://www.csvr.org.za/publications/1571-women-the-military-and-militarisation-some-questions-raised-by-the-south-african-case

10 T Modise and R Curnow (2000) 'Thandi Modise, a woman in war', *Agenda* 43: 36–40, p. 37,

http://www.sahistory.org.za/sites/default/files/thandi_modise.pdf

11 T Modise and R Curnow (2000) 'Thandi Modise, a woman in war', p. 39.

12 R Suttner (2011) 'Of masculinities and liberation', *Sunday Independent*, 12 December 2011, http://www.iol.co.za/sundayindependent/of-masculinities-and-liberation-1196880

13 B Goldblatt & S Meintjes (1996) 'Gender and the Truth and Reconciliation Commission: A submission to the Truth and Reconciliation Commission', May 1996, http://www.justice.gov.za/trc/hrvtrans/submit/gender.htm

14 B Goldblatt & S Meintjes (1996) 'Gender and the Truth and Reconciliation Commission: A submission to the Truth and Reconciliation Commission'.

15 O S Mngqibisa (1993) Sexual abuse of young women in the ANC camps. *Searchlight South Africa* 3(11): 14.

16 P Worsnip (2008) 'U.N. categorizes rape as a war tactic', Reuters, 20 June 2008, http://uk.reuters.com/article/uk-un-women-idUKN1948590120080620

17 L Vogelman & S Lewis (1993) 'Gang rape and the culture of violence in South Africa', Centre for the Study of Violence and Reconciliation, http://www.csvr.org.za/publications/1631-gang-rape-and-the-culture-of-violence-in-south-africa

18 For a full transcript of the judgment quoted in this book, see http://www.saflii.org/za/cases/ZAGPHC/2006/45.pdf

19 IOL News (2006) 'Zuma's accuser recounts her ordeal', 6 March 2006, http://www.iol.co.za/news/south-africa/zumas-accuser-recounts-her-ordeal-268431

20 A Meldrum (2006) 'Sobbing witness accuses Zuma of rape', *The Guardian*, 7 March 2006, https://www.theguardian.com/world/2006/mar/07/southafrica.andrewmeldrum

21 PD Gqola (2015) *Rape: A South African nightmare*. Johannesburg: Jacana Media, p. 144.

22 HS Bracha (2004) 'Freeze, flight, fight, fright, faint: adaptationist perspectives on the acute stress response spectrum', *CNS Spectrums* 9(9): 679–685, p. 679.

23 M Motsei (2007) *The kanga and the kangaroo court: Reflections on the rape trial of Jacob Zuma*. Johannesburg: Jacana Media, p. 15

24 Ibid., p. 14

25 Twitter, 6 August 2016, https://twitter.com/pierredevos

26 B Mthombothi (2016) 'Heed women's message about a president beyond shame', *Sunday Times*, 14 August 2016, https://www.pressreader.com/south-africa/sunday-times/20160814/282080571234628

27 News24 (2014) 'Judge questions Zuma rape verdict', 8 August 2014, http://www.news24.com/SouthAfrica/News/Judge-questions-Zuma-rape-verdict-20140808; and, later, in response to his claim of having been misquoted in the News24 article, S Evans (2014) 'Yacoob: I did not say I would have found Zuma guilty of rape', *Mail & Guardian*, 8 August 2015, https://mg.co.za/article/2014-08-08-yacoob-i-did-not-say-i-would-have-found-zuma-guilty-of-rape

28 For the full text of Zuma's statement, see http://www.politicsweb.co.za/party/zumas-2006-apology-following-rape-acquittal

29 E Lewis and A Makinana (2009) 'Accuser "enjoyed sex with Zuma"', IOL News, 23 January 2009, http://www.iol.co.za/news/politics/accuser-enjoyed-sex-with zuma-432215

30 Staff Reporter (2010) 'Malema guilty of hate speech', *Mail & Guardian*, 15 March 2010, https://mg.co.za/article/2010-03-15-malema-guilty-of-hate-speech

31 PD Gqola (2015) *Rape: A South African nightmare*. Johannesburg: Jacana Media, p. 153

CPSIA information can be obtained
at www.ICGtesting.com
Printed in the USA
BVOW10s1640191017

498150BV00030B/1484/P